MANAGEMENT INFORMATION SYSTEM

MANAGEMENT INFORMATION SYSTEM

PROF. RAMESH CHANDRA

KALPAZ PUBLICATIONS
DELHI–110052

MANAGEMENT INFORMATION SYSTEM

(Management)

Rs. 790

ISBN: 81-7835-142-0

Published in 2002 in India by
Kalpaz Publications
C-30, Satyawati Nagar
Delhi-110052
E-mail: kalpaz@hotmail.com

Laser Typesetting at: A.S. Printers
Printed at: Mehra Offset Printers, New Delhi

Contents

Preface

We are now living in a virtual age which may give rise to a paradoxical world where things seem both true and false. Technology may taken us faster, richer and smarter, but also alienated and materialistic. In the new digital age everything is destined to revolve around information technology, be it man or machine. The fax machines, electronic mails, and browsers are all working too well, faithfully feeding us with more and more information every day. Information technology has been an unambiguous virtue as a means of sustaining and developing culture.

People gather information directly by observing and experiencing events but as organisations become larger and more complex it becomes impossible for management, particularly in the middle and higher levels, to observe or experience all operations. In some forms of decentralised organisation management virtually never see the actual events and have to relay almost entirely on information provided through formal and informal channels. It is an information system using formalised procedures to provide managers at all levels in all functions with appropriate information from all relevant sources to enable them make timely and effective decisions for planning, directing and controlling the activities for which they are responsible.

This book offers a comprehensive analysis of management information system. It will serve as a complete reference tool to students, policy-makers, business managers.

Editor

1

Information System: An Introduction

If maximization of profit is accepted as a prime object of business, then a management information system sets out to quantify the profit objectives into the several shades of meaning, taking into account such constraints as resources, markets and timing. It further tries to interpret such objectives into meaningful figures and facts which are controllable by each specific level of management in each specific industry, company, function etc. Such objectives can then be analysed into periods of time, e.g. weeks, months, years, etc.

The next stage is the monitoring of results against these set objectives. At each periodic interval when comparison is made between the set objectives and the real results, a forward projection can be made to give an indication of profit.

Profit planning, and subsequent profit indication reporting give the basis of cash flow planning and cash flow reporting. At top level this information can be used as the basis of assessing funds required, return on capital and the effect capital expenditures will have on the performance of the company or group as a whole. So far a management information system has been described in its technical sense. If the philosophy of a company is that employees are the company then the management information system sets out in its wider sense to influence and motivate these people into being emotionally involved in the prosperity, profitability and continuity of the company.

Accountancy personnel are usually responsible for the mechanics of a management information system. If a management information system is to function to its fullest capacity, accountants must accept that they are the interpreters and summarizers of such information. They have to use their numerical skill to quantify the facts, hopes and problems of the various levels of management and as a result and problems of the various levels of management and as a result they are probably in a position to get the best overall view of their group or company. However, the best information systems are those in which the facts become self evident to each level of management whilst giving top management data as to where the strength and weaknesses lie. In this way, each manager and perhaps many employees can be businessmen working for the benefit of their company and able to measure their own contribution.

Consider a company or group in the form of a triangle or pyramid with the chairman and his board of directors at the top, and the various companies or sections of the business working down to the wider base. Within each section or company a similar triangle or pyramid can be built up.

At the top level, planning ahead for profit can be done as a broad concept in relation to previous years' profits, acquisitions, national and international climates, markets, capital expenditure and so on. At this state a broad idea of the level of profit can be assessed in relation to such factors as competition. This may be called a 'top to bottom' assessment.

At the base of pyramid individual employees and managers forming sections and companies, can make assessments in the field as to the performance that each section and ultimately the company can achieve in a similar time scale. Here each manager uses his own experience and knowledge in arriving at his answer. Comparison between the 'top to bottom' concept arrived at by he top management and the 'bottom to top' figures arrived at the summarizing the various assessments produced by the managers,can then be compared. At this stage identification of difference and why they occur can be more carefully examined.

The preparation of the detail by the individual managers and the subsequent examination of their findings is a means of involving them in the success or failure of the business as a whole.

the final summary of all the figures can be shown for the company as the one single objective expressed as a total profit in any one year or number of years.

The triangle or pyramid

Just as the preparation of this single profit objective is built up through the various tiers in the pyramid, information travelling up or down the pyramid can be summarized, to give comparison at each level. If the majority of managers are allowed to see the formation of targets, and the subsequent reporting and profit indications as time goes on, they can also see how their success or failure has strengthened or weakened the business as a whole. the pyramid in numerical terms envisages as the summarized answer a single total profit objective for any period of time which can be broken down into the several pars as we reach each level of management, section or employee. It is as well to emphasize that such figures do not only represent profit performance in accounting terms but can be broken down into efficiency ratios, sales per outlet, and all the other figures that would be meaningful to each discipline within the pyramid.

Setting up a system—targets and budgets

After the general concept of information systems is accepted then comes the task of putting a system into practical operation. How can this be started?

There exists in any business a financial accounting system, probably working along traditional historical reporting lines. There also usually exists at each management level formal or informal data which is used by individual management as their measure of performance. Some of it could be described as 'back of the envelope' assessment. These two things should be drawn together and formalized. This could perhaps begin by a company using historical figures of sales and expenses, working on the premise that if sales increase and expenses are controlled then profit will also increase. This can be called the naive approach.

Sales should be related to geographical areas and groups of people, and each level of management should examine details of these figures. Sales mix, gross margin analysis, etc. can be considered in detail, as can individual employee performances.

For each company the approach will be different. On the whole, however, it seems better to get more general targets started rather than become involved in too much detail too soon. Detail and individual commitment can become later at a stage when general reports are fed back, broken down at manager level and examined in detail.

Early detail before a grasp of what will be meaningful can waste time because line managers to be cynical as to the benefit or credibility of targets.

Each controllable item should be examined in detail with the people who are best able to control them. the method of the build up of such figures usually requires accounting assistance: the number of people; the number of vehicles; the load per vehicle; the amount of electricity used; the amount of water used; and so on. Identification of the major expense items and the setting of detailed calculated targets for these, whilst using a more general or historical base for the less significant items, is usually the best basis on which to found a system. The comments about too much detail too soon are again relevant.

There are only two ways to make a profit in business:

1. Increase gross margins
2. Reduce expenses

Having applied this theory to get some information flowing, there should follow almost immediately, examination of this information by each level of management in the light of performance, external comparison, commonsense, business hunch, or whatever, at suitable periodic intervals.

As a result calculations to quantify performance will begin to move away from the naive historical basis into more precise measurements of present achievable figures. Two examples will illustrate the point.

The sales of item 'x' last year were one million. A company's share of the market was 10%. National figures shows a general trend to a 3% increase. The gross margin attracted was 25%. From this data a simple target performance for the sale of 'x' can be set -e.g. 5% on last year's sales.

Actual performance figures as each week goes by might show that sales of 'x' show a 10% increase, although gross margins are only 18%.

Sales managers should analyse their sales and gross margins with the help of accounting staff into geographical areas, depots and perhaps individual salesmen. Discussion of these facts at meetings will begin to give information on new outlets or build up areas, saturated areas, special discount and promotion that erodes gross margin, wastage, etc. From this process could emerge:

(a) A deeper understanding of how figures are built up and therefore the true basis for setting meaningful targets.

(b) Education of management and employees as to the effect on overall figures that decisions in isolation have on performance, e.g. enthusiasm for getting sales volume up by promotion or special discount being nullified by reduction in total gross margin.

At this stage too identification of short and longer term objectives can begin. Setting constraints as to the amount that should be allowed in the short term to seek more sales at the subordination of gross margin should be more readily accepted.

Expenses—wages

Last year the wages for daily distribution in milk depot amount to Y thousand pounds. Wages increased from 1 April last year by 5%. There is a scheduled increase in April next year and under the Government's pay policy 6% will be allowed. This data can give a total answer for initial use in a naive budget.

On more detailed examination the calculation should be made as follows: The Deport has 10 milk rounds. Distribution is daily seven days per week. this gives 10 x 7 = 70 man days per week. Milkmen work a 5 day week.

Therefore 70/5 = 14 men required, i.e. 10 milkmen and 4 rota men.

Each man is entitled to 15 working days holiday per year.

On average each man is away 5 working days on sick leave per year.

The number of days of working lost = (15 + 5) x 14 = 280 days.

The calculation of weekly overtime per man to compensate = 280/52 x 14 days at overtime rates.

Given the weekly basis wage, overtime rates, etc. a weekly target wage bill can then be worked out to include this overtime factor.

Further sophistication could include cost of staff turnover, etc. on a similar basis.

So far the suggested development of information has taken place with income and expense being treated separately with involvement of the people best able to influence or control at that level. Much of the work here is the formalization of information from the various informal bases and sources. The next level of management should consider this information together, i.e. gross margin less expenses equals profit. From the initial assessment of such performance will stem other considerations:

1. Is the profit enough in relation to capital invested? last year? competition? etc.

2 What capital expenditure needs to be spent:

   (a) to maintain the present profit level?

   (b) to extend the profit level and with what return?

   (c) improve productivity?

3 Can the cash generated support the present capital expenditure plans?

Management information at this stage might be considered in two areas:

1. Information produced on a conceptual basis which sets out to answer 'what - if' questions. This may take the form of project investigations, e.g. if XYZ thousand pounds is spent on improving or rationalizing production, what savings can be made and what profit/spare capacity can be achieved?

2. Information drawn from acceptable figures of sales/ gross margin and expenses, which can be used as a basis for simple rules to assist in the daily/weekly assessment of performance, e.g. if a retail van sales distribution network were being considered then:

   (a) The direct expenses of a van could be worked out.

   (b) The basic wage could be calculated to include relief and holiday pay, etc.

(c) When the gross margin less commission or other variable reductions (e.g. discount) is equal to (a) plus (b) this gives a break even point prior to any contribution to overhead.

(d) If the overheads made up of depot administration and other costs are calculated then a figure of sales value per van per week can be established, which will be the lowest base of a weekly sales target figures, e.g. L450 sales per van per week.

At his stage a depot supervisor or van salesman knows that unless he can sell L450 per van per week his depot is not in profit. Consideration of sales mix, gross margin, value of sale per drop, etc. can then follow at a second stage investigation.

Setting up a system—reporting

Budgets or targets are the first part of the information system. To be effective there must be a continuous measurement against such targets at fairly short intervals. The determination of the interval of time depends on the level of management and the lead time for action to effect change. If an information system supplies too much information too often it will be just as ineffective as one which supplies no information at all.

As a general rule, the lower down the pyramid, or the nearer the manager to the immediate action, then more frequent but fewer facts and figures usually rove most useful. Conversely, top management need to take the longer term view when time should be allowed to see the effect that policy decisions produce.

Income and expenditure

Budgets and targets are based on profits broken down into periods. If figures are required (say) weekly, how are payments or receipts that cover a longer period of time dealt with? In simple terms they have to be smoothed so that the report shows profit and not merely cash balance at a point in time. Perhaps a few examples will illustrate the point.

1. Insurance. This may be paid annually inadvance on January 18th. If weekly reporting is envisaged a simple 1/52nd as an expense item in the management accounts can be shown.
2. Repairs. In considering a budget for repairs, it may be broken down into two groups:

   (a) Continuous or recurring maintenance, e.g. certain consumables, planed service, etc.

   (b) Special items of major replacement, e.g. a new boiler, generator, etc.

At this stage, when a budget total is established, a simple 1/52nd will give a weekly charge.

As the expenditure is incurred it can be classified in either category (a) or (b) above. If category (a) then each week's expenditure added to the cumulative and compared to budget will give an immediate indication of the adequacy of the estimate. Where the accumulated figure remains in excess of the accumulated budgeted figure then the weekly charge must be increased.

If the expenditure is in category (b) then a single comparison of the actual cost of the special item to the budgheted cost will give an over or under provision which can be divided by the remaining weeks in the year to increase or reduce the charge.

There is one further possibility. If at anytime a major item of expenditure occurs which is not budgeted , what then? One method is to smooth the expenditure forward by dividing it by the remaining weeks in the year. There are advocates of both methods.

Method I lends itself to those who want to see the special circumstance as an exception.

Method II gives a charge which, from that point onwards, will influence the weekly profit until the end of the year at the same rate. Profit projections forward are then more easily made for a group of companies.

A model developed below explicitly identifies and relates some factors which may determine when decisions are affected by accounting systems and information. The hypotheses on which this model is based are intended to stimulate and direct part of the study of accounting and decision-making. While the model is not tested here, some implications of the hypothesized relationships for both accounting theory and accounting systems are discussed.

The problems that demand new research in behavioral aspects accounting are familiar to almost all who have studied economics and accounting. The relationship between available information and decision is basic to economic theories of decision-making. Knowledge about costs, prices, and competitors is assumed in almost all traditional theory, and much effort has been directed toward developing models of decision-making for use when information about one or more of these factors is unknown. As these models have been explored and modified, and as new procedures for analysis of alternative courses of action have been developed, new attention has been given to the role of data as determinants of decisions.

Accounting systems of firms are important sources of information for business decision-making.

The information which systems provide for decision-making can be grouped in three classes: financial statements,quantitative reports on selected aspects of operations, and special analyses. Information from each class can be grouped with information from another or with information from sources outside the accounting system in the set of information used by a decision-maker. Almost all accounting information is affected by the body of rules and procedures called generally accepted accounting principles.

Efforts to develop and improve generally accepted accounting principles have been underway since the 1930's, and since 1960 these efforts have found vigorous support from the accounting profession. Thus far, these efforts have not been notably successful, for there are few, if any, bases on which all accountants can agree to select among alternative general principles. It is possible that much of the effort directed toward resolution of controversy about generally accepted accounting principles has been premature or misdirected.

Accounting is a service activity carried out to provide information for decisions within and about business firms. Analyses of alternative sets of generally accepted accounting principles have often been based on the assumption that the relationship between an accounting report or information contained therein and each decision is direct. But this assumption has not been tested, and alternative hypotheses abound. When these have been tested and efforts to develop generally accepted accounting principles can be based upon knowledge of the manner in which accounting affects decisions about business activity, new and important criteria for selecting among alternative methods and alternative systems will be available.

Accounting systems and information

One complication in the task of relating accounting information to decision-making is the fact that "accounting systems" are diverse and "accounting information" describes many different sets of data and information. For purposes of this paper, an "accounting system" will refer to the methods by which financial data about a firm or its activity are collected, processed, stored and/or distributed to members of the firm or other interested parties. It is possible to consider that any data or information which are obtained from or created in the accounting system of a firm are accounting information, whether contained in a financial statement, a special report, or verbal statement. However, for our immediate purposes, that interpretation is too broad to be useful. Hereafter, "accounting information" will refer to written information of the type that might be contained in a complete or partial financial report-balance sheet, income statement, or funds flow statement-though in many cases this limitation is not critical to the discussion.

By definition, decisions affect future events, for future actions are determined as a decision is made. In the case of management decisions, decisions may affect only a single event or they may affect all events subsequent to the decision. But no event which has been completed can be altered by a decision. Furthermore, accounting information, in the sense that we are using that term here, focuses on past events. Accounting cannot change events or their effects unless it is through the decision process where future events and their effects are determined. Decision-making and accounting information focus on different time periods except to the extent that the decision process employs accounting information. An important question then is, when is accounting information relevant for decision-making?

In a recent paper, Ijiri, Jaedicke, and Knight have provided a framework which is extremely useful as a basis for discussing the relationship of accounting information and decision processes. They represent a decision process as a function that relates a set of decision inputs to a unique set of decisions. Symbolically,

Here z_2, z_2,...., z_n are set of decisions based upon inputs, x_1 , x_2,....,x_n, according to a decision rule, h. Each set Z and X, must contain at least one element, but there is no requirement that the number of inputs be equal to the number of decisions.

Selection of a particular decision rule by a decision-maker is affected by many factors, among them his analytical capabilities and objectives. The rule associates inputs with decisions and selection of a decision rule establishes the degree to which objectives will be met by the expected effects of a particular set of decisions. The decisions-maker explores the relationships between decisions and objectives prior to the selection of a rule by analysis and through evaluation of the effects of past events similar to those contemplated in the future.

If accounting information affects decisions, it does so through a decision rule which relates decisions to inputs, which include accounting information. The decision-maker uses or selects a decision rule which relates inputs to decisions in a manner consistent with his experience, perceptions, and his objectives. Suppose we let x_1 represent consistent accounting information, one element of a set of all decision inputs available at the time a set of decisions is to be made. The decision rule weights each decision input. which determines each decision in the set Z, and the weight assigned to x_1 will determine what effect, if any, accounting information has on decisions affecting future events. All other decision inputs, x_2 through x_m are also weighted by the decision rule, and each affects the resulting set of decisions. These inputs may provide nonfinancial information essential to decisions, and in some cases their weights will overwhelm any possible effects of accounting information.

In selecting a decision rule, the decision-maker must consider all inputs available and their relevance to the set of decisions to be made. It is the decisions-maker who decides whether any input is relevant or not. The perceived relevance of the decision inputs to the decisions at hand determine whether the decision rule selected will apply a weight different from zero to accounting information. If a weight different from zero is applied, accounting information may affect decisions; if not, decisions will not be affected by accounting information. Therefore, we hypothesize: if accounting information is perceived as irrelevant for the set of decisions to be made, accounting information will not affect decisions; if accounting information is perceived as relevant to the set of decisions to be made, it may affect decisions.

Accounting is a systematic process of providing information about wealth and the effects of economic events. The methods, rules, and procedures that comprise accounting are here assumed to be familiar to the reader. However, there are reasons to believe that accounting is different things to different participants in economic events, and if so, the conceptions of accounting held by individuals or organizations may influence the impact of accounting information on behavior.

Away from reality, accounting can be regards as a perfect measure. A perfect measure can be defined as a measure where there is a zero probability that the true measurement of an attribute differs from the reported measurement. We can assume that identifiable objects and legal rights have value and that these values are enhanced or destroyed as economic events occur, and we can assume that these values and effects are measurable. To many persons, accounting practice, carried out by trained observers applying consistent and objective methods of measurement and attested to by independent agents, holds the image of a perfect measure applied buy professionals. There is an aura of authenticity that surrounds accounting data, and to the untrained user of information, accounting may appear to be a perfect source. We must recognize, however, that few, if any, of the persons who have processed or reviewed the data and the procedures that have converted it to information would consider it perfect.

More realistically, accounting can be considered as a process by which the value or effects of events is reported as a accurately as possible but without pretense of being a perfect measure. Here, this conception of accounting will be referred to as an "imperfect measure". Such a measure is defined when the probability that the true value differs from the reported value is greater than zero. This conception is probably closest to that held by most practicing accountants. Errors and inaccuracy in the process of measuring, counting, and reporting are inevitable, and most persons who are familiar with accounting measures and procedures are familiar with these problems. This notion may cause accounting to have a different impact on behavior than the "perfect measure" notion. It allows for a "margin of disbelief" that may in some cases affect the kind of action taken as accounting information is used in decision processes.

A third conception of accounting is fundamentally different from the "perfect measure" or "imperfect measure" notions advanced above. Accounting information may be a goal for actors in economic events. When a businessman seeks profit, he does so for many reasons. For some purposes, the profit reported by accounting is far more important to the businessman or manager than the "true" or "perfectly measured" profit. Modern business organization has given this conception of accounting wide significance, and the implications of this notion for accounting warrant close examination.

Accounting becomes a goal when rewards or satisfactions accrue to a decision-maker as a result of accounting informations, and the relationship of the true measure to the reported measure is unimportant. For example, if a manager hopes to advance and feels he will be promoted if he can effect cost reductions, and if accounting information will provide the basis for determining whether costs have been reduced, then it is the accounting information which shows reduced costs that becomes the goal. Likewise, where management is rewarded by stockholders with salary and prerequisites on the basis of reported earnings or growth, the reports which result in these rewards may become more important-the goal of management decision-makers-than the long-run earnings or healthy growth which the stockholders really intend to reward.

While not exclusive, this brief recognition of diverse conceptions of accounting seems essential to understanding the effects of accounting information on behavior and decision-making. Below it will be assumed that any individual in a decision situation conceives accounting information either as a goal or at a point on a continuum on which accounting varies from a perfect measure to an imperfect one. This assumption is necessary to state a second set of hypotheses relating accounting information and decisions: the conception of accounting held by a decisions-maker will affect his selection of a decision rule to be used in reaching a set of decisions. This hypothesis can be further specified by stating it in two parts:

1. If accounting information is both a decision input and an objective sought by a decision-maker, accounting information will affect decisions.
2. The more a decisions-maker conceives accounting as being a perfect source of information, the more likely the decision-maker will select decision rules that weight accounting heavily, and the more likely accounting information will affect decisions.

Classifying decisions-makers

Because accounting information can be conceived as a goal, and because accounting information is determined in part by an accounting system, a classification of decisions-makers provides insight into a final effect which accounting information may have on the set of decisions selected by the decisions-makers. Three classes are suggested; first, decisions-makers within the firm who make decisions both about operations and about the accounting system used to prepare reports; second, decision-makers within the firm who can make operating decisions but who cannot affect the methods used to prepare reports; and third, those outside of the firm who make decisions about the firm which may affect its environment and operations but who have no direct control over the operation of the firm or any activities in which it is engaged. The reasons for separating the first two classes of decision-makers, both of which are internal to the firm, will later become more obvious.

The first class of decision-makers is comprised of top management. Financial reports are the reports of this group and they are responsible for their preparation and presentation. If a choice must be made between accounting methods, this group is responsible for making that decision. This means that the set of possible decisions available to this class of decision-makers includes modification of the accounting system.

The second class of decision-makers is distinguished from the first only in one important way. Their position in the organization precludes their determining the information included in accounting reports by modifying the accounting system. However, they make decisions about the activities of the firm and we can assume that accounting information enters into their decisions processes. They can, of course, influence the content of accounting information by their decisions about activities. In which case accounting information may be affecting decisions.

The distinction between top management, who may affect accounting information, and internal decision-makers who cannot, is most critical where accounting information is conceived as a goal. The decision function for such managers may contain important options between operating decisions and decisions to change the methods by which accounting information is prepared. In any event, decisions are affected, but predicting directions of the effects is much more complicated than it is for decision-makers who do not have authority to modify accounting methods or procedures. Requirements for independent audits and certification of consistency in methods between accounting periods reduces the significance of the two levels of management, though few would argue that this requirement is such that the effects of top management's discretion in accounting can be ignored.

The third class of decision-makers consists of several sets of interested outsiders. Investors, legally the owners of the firm but in fact usually somewhat removed from it, are ostensibly the group for which accounting information in published form is prepared. Creditors, in some cases merely another class of investors, usually seek the same information. A third major set of outsiders consists of government agencies who seek bases for taxation, regulation, and economic analysis. Each of these sets of outsiders makes decisions that may affect the firm and its operations, and to the extent that accounting information is utilized as part of their decision processes, it will affect these decisions. However, the goals of the decisions-makers external to the firm presumably may differ from the objectives of the firm or objectives which concern decision-makers within the firm. This possibility makes analysis of effects of accounting information on decisions of this class of decision-makers very difficult.

Nevertheless, the classification of decision-makers yields an important hypothesis: if a decision-maker can affect the accounting system as well as the activities of the firm, and if he conceives accounting information as a goal, accounting information will affect decisions about either or both the accounting system and operations.

Non-accounting information

The final hypothesis to be introduced in this model concerns the role played by information which is not a product of the accounting system in determining the impact of accounting information on decisions. Above, accounting information was defined as information of the type that might be contained in a conventional financial report. In many respects, the effects of non-accounting information on decisions can be analyzed in the same framework as accounting information. However, the importance of non-accounting information here is that it may determine the effects of accounting information on decisions.

If non-accounting information becomes a goal or is perceived as having special relevance for decisions undergoing evaluation, the impact of accounting information will be reduced. If non-accounting information is not relevant to decisions, the effects of relevant accounting information will be enhanced. Therefore, we hypothesize: the impact of accounting information on decisions is affected by the perceived relevance of other information also available to the decision-maker.

The hypotheses developed above are all summarized and their interrelationships are made clear. Rather than restate all hypotheses or describe the model in detail, a summary of hypotheses which lead to the principal outcomes predicted by the model will be used to reveal the interrelationships within it.

1. Accounting information will either affect decisions or affect decisions about the accounting system if:
   (a) accounting information is relevant to decisions; and
   (b) the decisions-maker conceives accounting as a goal;
   (c) the decisions-maker is a member of the firm who can control the selection and operation of the accounting system.

II. Accounting information will affect decisions if:
   (a) accounting information is relevant to decisions;
   (b) the decision-maker conceives accounting as a goal; and
   (c) the decision-maker is a member of the firm who cannot control the selection and operation of the accounting system;
   (c2) the decisions-maker is external to the firm;or
   (b2) the decision-maker conceives accounting as a perfect measure;
   (c) non-accounting information is not relevant to the decision.

III. Accounting information may affect decisions if;
   (a) accounting information is relevant to decisions;

(b1) the decision-maker conceives accounting as a perfect measure; and

(c) non-accounting information is relevant to the decision;

(b2) the decision-maker conceives accounting as an imperfect measure; but

(c) non-accounting information is not relevant to the decision.

IV. Accounting information will not affect decisions if:

(a1) accounting information is not relevant to decisions; or

(a2) accounting information is relevant to the decisions; but

(b) the decision-maker conceives accounting information as an imperfect measure; and

(c) non-accounting information is relevant to the decision.

The model predicts that accounting information perceived as perfect may have some effect on decisions. However, when the decision-maker perceives accounting information as being something less than perfect, the impact of other information becomes less certain. The degree of conceived imperfection and the amount and quality of other information are important variables in such cases. Likewise, even in cases where accounting information is perfect, and other information is relevant, the decision might be affected, but not altered, by accounting information. Similar questions can be raised at other points and simply reinforce conclusions about the need for testing the hypotheses on which this model is based.

While these uncertain conclusion beg for clarification and discriminating research, they are perhaps the least interesting. In cases where decisions may be little affected by accounting information, the choice of a particular accounting system, or particular accounting methods used in that system, may be of little importance. It is at the other extreme, where the model predicts that accounting information will affect decisions that the choice of accounting systems and methods becomes critical.

Further complications in interpreting or using the model stem from possible interaction between the method of accounting used and/or the accounting system developed and the perceived relevance of accounting for decision-making purposes. If the decision-maker feels that a particular method or system of accounting is inappropriate as a basis foe measurements relating to a particular problem, he will be led to a position where the effective accounting information will be reduced. Unless we know something about the particular class of decision-makers and their perceptions of accounting methods, it is difficult to predict whether any examination of the conception of accounting held by the decision-maker will be of importance. Likewise, if the method chosen, or the process of selecting a method, affects the conception of accounting held by the decision-makers, then this will affect the relationship between a particular method and decisions.

The proposal made here to recognize relevance as a primary determinant of the effect of accounting on decision-making is not new. The degree of relevance has frequently been suggested as a basis for choosing between alternative accounting methods and forms of accounting information. This has been particularly true in the literature relating to accounting within the firm, where it is frequently asserted that those methods that result in revelation of cost-volume-profit relationships are most appropriate. Likewise, in the recent Statement of Basic Accounting Theory, formulated by a committee of the American Accounting Association, relevance is proposed as a primary standard for selecting among alternative forms of accounting information. However, the meaning of relevance appropriate for its use as a criterion in the development of accounting methodology and theory is not clear. While users are frequently the point of reference in analyses employing "relevance", the determination of "relevant information" is left to the accountant, who uses some standard, generally accepted model for decision-making as the criterion in determining what should be reported. In the formulation which has been presented above, relevance is determined by the user of the information, and the effect of this choice creates several problems which require careful consideration before this criterion is employed. If the user determines relevance, we should expect that, in some cases, what the user feels is relevant would not be relevant in those standard, accepted models with which we are familiar, such as those drawn from economics.

Suppose the accountant knows the objectives of the firm and those objectives correspond to those in an accepted model of decision-making, but the decision-maker feels the relevant information is different from that called for by the model. The accountant may be placed in a position of second guessing the user, in order to provide the data that will allow him to make a correct decision, because the user's idea of what information is relevant is wrong from the standpoint of the decision models. This is a position in which I believe most accountants would feel somewhat uncomfortable.

We must also be concerned with the possibility that the conception of accounting held by the decision-maker affects the perception of relevance to a significant degree. The more a decision-maker conceives of accounting as being perfect, the more relevant accounting information is likely to be for decision-making purposes, and the more importance can be attached to the part that accounting systems and methods will play in the decision-making process. In so far as this writer is aware, this relationship has seldom been considered, and never carefully explored.

If the hypotheses developed in this paper are valid, then it is clear that relevance alone cannot serve as a primary standard for the development of accounting theory and methods. If accounting is to serve users of accounting information then something besides whether or not the data is relevant must be known. These hypotheses would lead us to believe that critical variables are the conception of accounting held by a decision-maker and the perceived relevance of other kinds of information to the problems under examination at the time the user chooses to employ or not to employ accounting information. Some examples of the use of relevance and the conception of accounting as bases for accounting systems development

Suppose that research fails to lead to rejection of the hypotheses presented above, and consider a case in which we are concerned with designing an appropriate accounting system to facilitate effective decision-making. Imagine that the organization in question is a business firm. Among the products of an accounting system are financial statements issued at regular intervals.

These intervals may vary in length from very short periods to relatively longer periods; that is, financial statements may be prepared for internal use as frequently as daily or weekly, or they may be issued less often, perhaps annually, to employees of the firm. It is possible to hypothesize that the more frequently financial reports are issued and attention is drawn to the financial condition of the firm, the more relevant accounting information will appear to people within the firm who are making decisions about prices, promotion policies, and production quantities. Yet, for many decisions of this type, we might argue that other information would be more important and relevant . Therefore, we might be led to situation in which we wish to reduce the perceived relevance of accounting information by reducing the frequency of reports, so that decision-makers within the firm would rely more heavily on other information which would allow their decisions to be more appropriate for the conditions under which the firm was operating. Consider pricing decisions. In general, economists and other analysts would agree that the financial condition of the firm is not necessarily an appropriate basis for choosing a price strategy and selecting terms of sale.

However, if financial statements are issued very frequently, thus enhancing their perceived relevance, and the conception of accounting held by decisions-makers is such that we might expect accounting information to have some effect, then favorable or adverse profit information and/or other financial information might affect decisions with respect to price. It is possible, then, that by developing an accounting system in which the frequency of reporting reduce the perceived relevance of accounting information we could improve pricing decisions in the firm.

In other cases, we might come to an opposite conclusion. In decision making related to the acquisition and management of working capital, the availability of frequent information on the status of assets and liabilities of the firm may be very important, and we might chose to issue reports to persons concerned with these matters very frequently in hopes of increasing the efficiency of such decisions.

The point of these examples is that changes in the accounting system may affect perceived relevance of accounting information and may determine the effect of accounting information on decisions, and furthermore, that the interactions between relevance and conceptions of accounting which we have considered above may be important also. In designing an accounting system, relying on cliches like ".... the more information, the better...." may lead to surprising results. Consider another example, in which we are concerned with a choice between alternative accounting methods for reporting on a particular class of assets or liabilities. For sake of illustration, let us consider a choice between two alternative inventory valuation methods-LIFO and FIFO.

Assuming that the reader is familiar with the characteristics of these methods, we can quickly conclude that in cases where prices are changing frequently that LIFO will reveal through the income statement the effects of these changes on the profitability of the firm more rapidly than FIFO. To the extent that this is important for the types of decisions being made, this model might provide us with the basis for preferring one method of accounting for inventories over another.

Let us assume that the prices of raw materials for the production process or the price of goods to be resold is rising. From the standpoint of decision-makers within the firm, this is important information, and information which we would expect to be important for decision-making purposes within the firm. To the extent that the decision-maker felt accounting information was relevant to his decisions, a conception of accounting as perfect information would make the choice of LIFO more important than if the decision-maker's conception of accounting information was that it was an imperfect measures. If accounting information is not perceived as relevant, or if the decision-maker feels accounting measures are imperfect and other information is also relevant for decision-making , the choice of inventory valuation methods is unlikely to affect decisions. Here also we can consider the possible usefulness of this model for evaluating the selection of a method for reporting to external users. Assume that external users feel accounting information is relevant for their decisions.

The more perfect their conception of accounting, the more likely that the choice between methods of accounting will affect their decisions. If the current performance of the firm is important to external users because they wish to use it as a basis for decisions, then LIFO may be more appropriate than FIFO for inventory valuation purposes.

In either of these last two cases. If accounting information were perceived as being irrelevant and/or if accounting information were conceived as being so imperfect a measure that it is not weighted heavily by the decision rule, then a decision on an inventory valuation method might not be very important. Such would be the case in any choice between accounting systems or methods. The implication of this is, I believe, quite clear: until we know more about the conditions that affect perceived relevance of accounting information for decision-making and until we know more about the conceptions of accounting held by users we do not have adequate bases on which to reduce diversity in accounting or to increase it selectively.

Implications for further research

It is clear that a great deal more research about behavioral relationships between accounting and decision-making is required. The hypotheses which comprise the model presented here demand that we learn more about the factors that influence a decision-maker's perception of the relevance of accounting information.

We need to know more about the conceptions of accounting held by individuals, both within business enterprises and external to them and it would be useful also to know more about the magnitudes of difference required before perceptions of relevance and conceptions would be affected.

One way of finding data about these variables would be to g into the field and do field research about the perceived relevance of accounting for various decision problems. Some attempts have been made in this direction, and while the results are still inconclusive, they provide a basis for the design of further studies. It is also necessary that something be learned about the conceptions of accounting held by users. Is it true that the majority of users feel accounting is a valid and good source of information? Or do most experienced users of accounting information conceive of accounting as being imperfect in the sense that the term is used here, and hence, the types of decisions made about accounting systems and accounting methods are relatively unimportant?

Another approach to this type of problem is the experimental approach, where in a laboratory or a simulated environment, we place people in alternative conditions in hopes of comparing their behavior under the conditions we have created. This, in my opinion, provides a most promising avenue for testing some of the hypotheses we have created in this study.

Consider, for example, an experiment to determine if the relevance of accounting information is a determinant of the effect of that information on decision-making. We could, for example, take a sample group and partition it to obtain a control section and an experimental section. The experimental section could be instructed as to the types of situations in which, given generally accepted models of decision-making, accounting information is relevant. Having provided this background, this group could then take part in a simulated exercise-a business game-in which accounting information and other information are controlled.

2

Management Concepts

This chapter discusses some important management concepts that underlie an organization's structural design. Those management concepts that are essential for accountants to understand in order to perform their information communication function effectively are emphazied. A company's accounting subsystem performs a service function of converting financially-oriented data into useful information. Consequently, the accounting subsystem can be referred to as the accounting information system. In this chapter, as well as later ones, accounting information system will therefore be used as a synonym for the accounting subsystem.

Accountants must thoroughly understand their organization's goals in order to make a positive contribution to their accomplishment. A goal basically represents what one is attempting to achieve. Most people, as well as organizations, have several goals. Ideally, the multiplicity of goals that employees and their organizations have should be in harmony with each other. The harmony among employees' goals and organizational goals is called goal congruence. This means that in the process of achieving personal goals, the individual employee also contributes toward accomplishing organizational goals. On the other hand, frustration can result when the positive achievement of one goal conflicts with other goals, which is called goal incongruence. This type of frustration occurs in both individuals and organizations.

Organization theory suggests that an individual usually joins a company for personal gain but, in the course of time, gradually learns to accept, and work toward, the company's goals. Both large and small businesses encourage such learning and acceptance of organizational goals by permitting employees to participate in developing these goals; by creating profit-sharing and employee professional improvement programs; by organizing social activities such as bowling leagues, picnics, and the like, which create the feeling of a working "family": and, in general, by making employees feel that it is their company.

Nevertheless, discord between personal goals and organizational goals still can occur. One example would be the individual's desire for promotion to an area for which he or she is not fully qualified. You might also recognize the above example as the "Peter principle"- a person is promoted to his or her level of incompetence. In such situations, the individual's goal of personal achievement conflicts with the organization's goal of increased operating efficiency. Other examples of conflict include personal location preferences versus organizational needs, and personal desires for more subordinates versus organizational policy on maximum supervision. For an organization's multiplicity of goals to be in harmony, the organization should consider its employees' needs when establishing these goals. The accounting information system plays a major role in providing relevant information to an organization's management regarding the establishment and eventual achievement of its specific goals. An important way to resolve conflict is by providing information about organizational operations.

The accounting information system attempts to provide this relevant information to each organizational subsystem(as well as to top management) so that the subsystems and top management can contribute positively to the company's goals, thereby avoiding goal conflict. The two major organizational goal categories are (1) nonoperational goals (normally long-range, broadly stated goals of top management) and (2) operational goals (normally short-range goals established by each subsystem to contribute positively toward accomplishing the nonoperational goals). We will now discuss each of these categories.

Two important managerial functions are planning and controlling. Most organizations perform both long-range and short-range planning. The former is normally the function of an organization's top management and is sometimes also called strategic planning. Through its long-range strategic planning, the organization develops a "plan of attack" for the future. The strategies established by top management are usually expressed in broad, nonoperational terms. For example, the long-range nonoperational goals developed by the Alan Company's top management.

1. A satisfactory level of net income.
2. A high quality of manufactured sporting goods.
3. A responsive and motivated group of employees.

4. A contribution to a clean environment through pollution control.

These goals are nonoperational because they are stated very broadly and reflect the long-range accomplishments desired by the Alan Company's top management.

Basically, a satisfactory income is below a maximizing income, which satisfies the various persons (the stockholders, the board of directors, etc.) associated with the specific organization. If management's profit performance fails to satisfy its stockholders, for example, many of the top managers may find themselves looking for other jobs.

Long-run profit maximization goal

There are three major reasons why most organizations strive for a satisfactory, rather than a maximizing, level of long-run net income. First, and probably most important, is the fact that a nonoperational goal of profit maximization would probably conflict with an organization's other nonoperational goals. Maximizing profits would require each of the specific nonoperational goals to also be directed towards profit. In many organizations, this dies not occur. Often, one or more of an organization's nonopertional goals actually run counter to increasing profits. For example, some of the employee benefit programs that the Alan Company institutes to achieve its nonoperational goal of a responsive and motivated work force may actually decrease the company's annual net income. Also, the additional expenditures incurred by the Alan Company in contributing to a clean environment will likely reduce profits. Thus, when an organization has a multiplicity of goals that are not all directed at increased profitability, considerable goal conflict could result if profit maximization were a goal. A satisfactory profit performance goal, however, should be in harmony with other organizational goals.

A second argument against profit maximization relates to an organization's difficulty in ascertaining its profit-maximizing performance level. Economists tell us that profit maximization occurs when an organization operates at the point where marginal revenue equals marginal cost. This theory sounds nice, but actually deriving the marginal revenue and marginal cost data for a specific company can be quite difficult, if not possible.

Third, if an organization attempted to develop a current year budget that incorporated a profit maximization goal, certain decisions may be made that actually harm long-run organizational performance. For example, within the Alan Company's marketing subsystem in a research and development component. Its function is to develop new and innovative products as well as improve the quality of current product lines. Because research and development costs represent operating expenses in the year of their incurence, the Alan Company's management could increase its 1988 income performance by reducing the current year's expenditures for research and development.

However, this decision could lead to reduced profits in future years if the company's competitors continue to develop new and improved products. The long-run effects of the Alan Company's attempt to maximize its short-run profits in 1988 might cause the company to obtain a smaller share of the future sporting goods sales market because of its competitors' superior products. This would obviously lead to a reduction of profits for the Alan Company in the long run.

Employees within the Alan Company's individual subsystems must thoroughly understand their company's long-range goals and attempt to contribute positively to these goals. Each subsystem is responsible for developing operational goals that will help accomplish the company's nonoperational goals. To achieve these nonoperational goals, employees from the various subsystems should communicate with one another so that their goals are in harmony, rather than in conflict. We will now examine the role played by the Alan Company's accounting information system in achieving the company's operational goals.

Accounting information system's role

The accounting information system's major contribution to the Alan Company's top-management nonoperational goals is the development of long-range as well as short-range operational budgets. Because budgets affect all organizational subsystems, the accountants must communicate with each subsystem's employees and seek their participation in planning, implementing, and controlling the budgetary system.

Budgeting (both long-range and short-range budgets) will be covered extensively. The purpose of briefly analyzing budgeting at this point is to show the accounting information system's major contribution to its organization's planning and controlling functions, which lead to the accomplishment of the organization's multiplicity of goals. In its short-range planning, assume that the Alan Company wishes to prepare the 1988 operating budget. The company's budget committee, including representatives from top management and each of the company's subsystems, meets in September of 1987. Because of accountants' training as financial experts, and because the budget is a financial projection, the company's managerial accountants on the budget committee are appointed as committee coordinators. In the process of developing the 1988 budget, the committee's job is to make operational the previously stated nonoperational goals of top management. Each subsystem's operational budget should contribute positively to these goals.

We will now discuss the accounting information system's specific role in aiding the accomplishment of the Alan Company's four nonoperational goals. Accounting Information System's Contribution to Nonoperational Goal to Satisfactory net Income Performance. The previously discussed arguments against profit maximization should be understood by the accountants when they perform their functions as budget coordinators.

Accountants on the budget committee must develop projected financial statements for 1988 that will guide the Alan Company toward satisfactory income performance. For example, in accumulating the data for the company's 1988 projected income statement budget, the accountants must develop the revenue and expense estimations with an understanding of top management's goal to achieve satisfactory rather than maximizing profits. One of the major expenses on a manufacturing firm's income statement is its "cost of goods sold" resulting from sales of manufactured inventory items.

When the accountants aid the production subsystem in developing its standard manufacturing costs for raw materials, direct labor, and production overhead, they should be aware of the company's goal of achieving satisfactory operating performance. Therefore, these standard manufacturing costs should be based on a reasonably efficient level of performance rather than a maximizing performance output. Once determined, the company's standard manufacturing costs for its various types of sporting goods inventory items would represent useful information to aid the development of the production subsystem's 1988 operating budget. In attempting to develop a satisfactory level of sales revenue for the 1988 income statement budget, the Alan Company's marketing subsystem must estimate the expected sales of the many sporting goods equipment product lines.

A sales mix represents the quantity combination of the many products an organization hopes to sell. To aid the marketing subsystem in determining this sales mix, the Alan Company's accounting information system can provide marketing with relevant information regarding the manufacturing costs associated with the various sporting goods product items.

The production subsystem has the primary responsibility for achieving this top-management goal. Production managers may hire quality control experts who inspect the manufactured sporting goods to make sure they meet the designated quality standards.

The accounting information system's major role concerning quality production would be financially justify the level of quality sporting goods desired by top management. To execute this function, the accountants would perform a cost/benefit analysis for the Alan Company's individual sporting goods products. Ideally, the benefits expected from each product line (i.e., the revenues that eventually will result from selling the specific product) should exceed the company's costs in manufacturing it. At a minimum, each product line should make a positive contribution margin (excess of selling price over variable manufacturing, selling price over variable manufacturing, selling, and administrative expenses) towards covering those fixed costs associated with the product. One of the important variable costs that affects the quality level of a company's manufactured product is the purchase price of the raw materials used in production.

The accountant's analysis of the raw materials costs that would be necessary to achieve top management's desired production quality level may indicate that the high-quality materials needed for production are too costly, resulting in a negative product line contribution margin (total variable costs exceed selling price). With this information, the accountant may recommend that top management decrease the quality level for the specific product line. This would enable the production subsystem to purchase a lower-cost raw material. By slightly altering the finished product's quality level, the company may be able to convert a negative product line contribution margin to a positive one.

Once an agreement is reached regarding the quality level of raw materials for each manufactured product line, the accountant can further contribute to top management's quality product goal through timely performance reports disclosing any significant variations between the actual quality of raw materials purchased and the quality level of raw materials that should have been purchased (based on the established quality standard). The subject of timely performance reports will be emphasized later in this chapter.

The personnel subsystem has the primary responsibility for achieving this goal. As a result of effective personnel selection procedures, adequate compensation, efficiently operating training programs, and the involvement of employees in challenging activities, the Alan Company's labor force should have positive attitude towards their work environments.

The accountants, in performing their cost accounting, budgetary, and systems study functions, must consider the human element within a company. Rather than just informing the employees what their budget allowances will be or unilaterally introducing a systems change, for instance, the accountants should seek the employees' participation in making these decisions. Employees should be more responsive and positively motivated to achieve their company's goals if they participate in various decisions affecting their work environments. Consider, the example, the process involved in developing the standard number of labour hours for manufacturing the Alan Company's many sporting gods product lines by the production subsystem. the accountants within the accounting information system would have a major role in developing these labor standards and subsequently reporting to management any significant variations between actual and standard labor hours.

If the standards for employee performance are too high, most production employees will be unable to attain them, causing management to evaluate the employees unfavorable. Obviously, this situation can lead to employee frustration. If, however, the accountants allow the production employees to participate in the development of the standards with the objective of setting the labor standards with the objective of setting the labor standards at a level that the "average" employee can achieve, the employees should feel that the standards are fairer. As a result, the employees should be more responsive and thus motivated to operate effectively under the standard cost system. Timely performance reports that compare actual with standard labor hours should motivate employees to perform favorably in relation to these "attainable" established standards. Further motivation can result from monetary and promotional benefits to those employees who perform favorably.

Another behavioral aspects of the accountants organizational duties concerns the design of subsystem managers' performance reports that fairly reflect each manager's contribution to top management's nonoperational goals. If a subsystem manager is evaluated on the basis of operating items over which he or she has no control, the individual may become frustrated. As will be emphasized later, the accountants can contribute to employee motivation by designing subsystem performance reports that evaluate each subsystem manager only on the manager's controllable operating activities. This is called a responsibility accounting system.

The Alan Company's production subsystem makes an important contribution to this goal by utilizing efficient machinery and equipment in its manufacturing process, thereby minimizing environmental pollution.

The accounting information system's role in achieving adequate pollution control would be directed toward helping management decide which of the many possible pollution-reducing approaches is economically most efficient. For example, assume that the Alan Company's present manufacturing equipment is causing a level of environmental pollution in excess of minimum government pollution standards. The accountants could perform an analysis of the expected costs versus the expected benefits to the Alan Company of either making its current manufacturing equipment more efficient or completely modernizing the production plant.

The benefits that the accountants would attempt to measure from each alternative include such things as reduced pollution, improved quality of manufactured products which would likely lead to increased sales of the company's sporting goods, and the estimated increase in sporting goods' sales resulting from the favorable public image created by the company's environmental pollution program. The accountants would recommend that pollution control alternative offering the greatest benefits in relation to its costs. Once management has reached a decision regarding which pollution program to undertake and has established its standard level of acceptable pollution, the accounting information system would provide pollution control variance reports.

These reports would compare the actual levels of pollution from the new program with the predetermined standard pollution levels, thereby informing manufacturing department managers and top management whether or not their pollution control program is operating effectively. The accounting information system's role in environment control is only part of an important area in the accounting profession called social reporting. Under this type of reporting, accountants attempt to measure the impact on society of various organizational activities, such as energy conservation and fair employment practices.

Upon establishing each subsystem's operational goals that will contribute to top management's nonoperational goals, a reporting structure is needed to ascertain whether or not the subsystem's planned operational goals are being achieved. Through the controlling function of timely reports comparing each subsystem's actual performance with its budgeted performance, those organizational areas that are operating inefficiently can be determined and necessary corrective action taken. This controlling function is extremely crucial because without such evaluation reports, top management as well as operating management would be unaware of a specific system's contribution to the nonoperational goals.

These internal parties include an organization's top management as well as the operational managers within each subsystem. Certain organizational communications are oral; however, a large amount of company's communications takes place through written reports. An extremely important type of written report is the performance report, which evaluates a subsystem's success or failure in accomplishing its operational goals. One of the major criteria for assessing a subsystem's achievement of its operational goals is the subsystem's actual performance compared with its predetermined budget. Because accountants are usually the coordinators of their organization's budgetary system, they have the important function of designing and communicating the organization's performance reports.

For these reports to fulfill their control objectives, they must have two characteristics. First, the reports should be timely so that a minimum period elapses between an activity and the feedback reflecting its actual performance. Second, the reports should provide relevant information to their recipients so that they can take the necessary action to accomplish the organization's goals.

To achieve these two characteristics in performance reports, the accountants work closely with EDP employees. The speed of a computer in processing data has enabled faster feedback of performance information to individual subsystems and top management. This allows a subsystem's managers to correct inefficiencies in shorter time following their occurrence. However, the computer's ability to process data quickly is unproductive to a company's decision making unless the data provided to the computer are relevant.

The data input stage is the principal link between the accounting information system and EDP. The accountants must understand the information needs of each manager in their organization in order to accumulate for computer processing the relevant data needed for effective decision making.

An important organizational concept is the delegation of authority by top management to the managers within each subsystem. In small organizations, this is often minimal because the owner is aware of everything the occurs in the organization and can make all the necessary decisions. However, in large organizations, it is impossible for one or a few top managers to keep abreast of all organizational activities and make timely decisions within the various subsystems. Size and complexity have been the major factor causing top management to delegate decision-making authority to lower level managers to that these organizations will function more efficiently. When a subsystem manager is given the authority to perform certain activities, this manager should also be held responsible for his or her actions. It should be emphasized, however, that in the final analysis, top management remains responsible for the actions of its subsystem managers in achieving the organization's goals. Responsibility cannot be delegated from one individual to another. For example, if a specific subsystem fails to accomplish its operational goals, the organization's stockholders will hold top management responsible for this inefficiency.

The accountants should be aware of the authority and responsibility relationships within their organization because each subsystem's performance report must be "tailor-made" to measure the success or failure of the subsystem to execute those function over which it has authority and responsibility.

In designing performance reports that provide relevant information regarding the positive or negative contribution of each subsystem toward achieving the organization's nonoperational goals, the accountants should utilize a responsibility accounting system. Under this type of reporting system, they must first analyze the authority and responsibility structure of their organization. Then, a reporting system is developed whereby each subsystem is evaluated only on those activities over which it has control. A controllable item is one that the subsystem can cause to change. By evaluating a subsystem's performance on the basis of activities that it can control, a fairer and truer picture of its operating performance is obtained. Only those operating items over which the subsystem has control and for which it is therefore responsible should be included in its budget. The subsequent evaluation of a particular subsystem's performance would include a comparison of the subsystem's actual controllable items with its budgeted controllable items. Any significant variations between actual results and budget projections would be the responsibility of that subsystem.

A control system is normally not effective unless one can traced to the specific subsystem that caused them, and corrective action can then be planned. Another important advantage of a responsibility accounting system is from a behavioral point of view. If a responsibility accounting system is not used, subsystems will often be evaluated on the basis of activities outside of their control. This can cause frustration to a subsystem's management. In many organizations, the accountants' performance report is the major criterion used by top management to evaluate a particular subsystem manager's effectiveness.

Think of yourself for a minute as the Alan Company's manager of the basketball manufacturing department. Version 1 is based on a responsibility accounting system, whereas version 2 includes cost items over which you have no control. Which of these two performance reports would you consider to be a truer picture of your effectiveness as basketball manufacturing department manager?

Assumes that the basketball manufacturing department has authority and responsibility for the dollar expenditures on raw materials, direct labor, and variable overhead utilized in production. Because the departments' actual controllable costs were $500 below the January budget get, you as the manager would likely receive a favorable evaluation ion the basis of the version 1 report, which evaluates this department's performance based on the monetary items it can control.

The version 2 performance report could make you somewhat frustrated. Here, monetary items over which you have no control are being charged to your budget and used to evaluate your subsequent performance. The end result is that your department's actual costs are $900 over the January budget, causing top management to look unfavorably at your department. The major factors causing the unfavorable performance were the three monetary items for which you had no authority and responsibility. For example, the $800 excess of allocated selling and administrative expenses over the budget may have been the result of overtime wages paid to administrative personal. This overtime may have been necessary because of careless and inefficient performances by some administrative employees. Naturally, if the Alan Company's top management executives received the version 2 report in and examined each line closely, they would see that your department performed successfully on its controllable financial items.

But, as is sometimes true, top management may look only at the bottom line, indicating a $900 net unfavorable operating performance. Because top management now considers your department inefficient during January, your morale and motivation may drop considerably due to the unfair basis of evaluation.

A common problem faced by many organizations having computerized management information systems is the massive quantity of data printed out by their computers. A company may intentionally create additional unnecessary reports just to feel it is obtaining full value from its expensive computer equipment. Another factor causing "excessive data reporting" is the status attached by many business managers to receiving internally generated reports. The more reports a manager receives, the greater importance the manager may attach to his or her role in an organization.

Whatever the causes of excessive reports may be, the result can often lead to inefficient decision making. If a subsystem manager is faced with a situation in which a quick decision is needed information had been readily available, the manager's final decision may have made a more positive contribution to achieving the company's goals. Along with designing a responsibility accounting system, the accountants can help reduce the massive number of reports flowing through a company's system by incorporating a management-by-exception reporting structure into their company.

The underlying assumption of management-by-exception is that if a specific operating activity is progressing according to plan, there is no reason to report this information to management. Only when a particular activity deviates significantly from the original plan should the information be immediately reported to the responsible manager so that necessary action can be taken. A management-by-exception reporting structure offers several advantages to a company.

First, it reduces the length and number of reports generated by the company's information system because reports are prepared only when significant operating deviations exist and include only information about these significant deviations. This advantage results in important cost savings because processing a report and communicating it through the system can be costly. Second, management-by-exception reporting reduces the amount of time that highly paid managers must spend reading reports. They will therefore have additional time to perform more productive functions. Third, and perhaps most important, the managers will receive reports only when it is essential for them to take action on some aspect of their specific subsystem exception report will thus direct a manager to actual operating functions that require immediate attention rather than to each of the subsystem's many activities, whether they need corrective adjustments or not.

What constitutes a significant variation from plan and should therefore be reported to management often involves subjective judgment. Accountants, with their understanding of an organization's financial operating activities, should have a valuable input to these decisions. To demonstrate the advantages of a management-by-exception reporting system, assume that a weekly computerized report goes to the Alan Company's marketing managers comparing this subsystem's actual sales with its budgeted sales.

The input for the report comes from each budget projections that the accounting information system helped develop. The format of this weekly report was designed by the company's accountants. Illustrates the Alan Company's sales report for the third week of January 1988. Imagine yourself as a manager in the Alan Company's marketing subsystem who reads this detailed sales report each week You may become frustrated and begin skimming the large volume of reports that cross your desk. This could cause you to overlook some relevant information that requires your immediate attention. If a management-by-exception reporting structure had been designed by the accountants, the weekly computer printout would not include all the data in but only those budget variations that were considered significant. For example, examining the total budget and total actual sales of golf balls, the 70 cartons under budget may not be considered significant. After a closer look at the individual causes of this variation, however, two significant facts are revealed. Mr. Baker's golf ball sales in region F were 250 cartons under budget, whereas Ms. Worthley's sales in region S were 100 cartons over budget. Under management-by-exception reporting, this information about Baker and Worthley's golf ball sales would be provided to marketing management. Information regarding any one of the Alan Company's other product-line regional sales whose budget variation for each product line in the various sales regions. Reflects the Alan Company's sales exception report for the third week of January 1988.

By comparing with it is obvious that the exception report will permit more efficient and effective decision making by the marketing managers. This exception report can be read faster than the complete sales data in, and, more important, it immediately discloses those budget variations that are significant. It is important to note that management-by-exception reports include both favorable and unfavorable budget variations. This reporting method can thus be a useful motivational device for recognizing superior employee performance.

For example, Ms. Worthley's 100 golf ball sales cartons over budget in region S would be fully recognized by her superiors. On the other hand, Mr. Baker's 250 golf ball sales cartons below budget in region F would be discussed with him and plans made for trying to increase this region's future golf ball sales.

The computer's role in management

Through communications among managers of the accounting information system, marketing, and EDP, decisions can be reached for each product line as to what constitutes a significant budget variation and therefore a reportable exception. Because budgets reflect future projections, it is quite unlikely that actual operating results will be identical with budget projections. Some budget variation should be expected solely because of random chance.

Let's assume that the Alan Company's marketing managers and its accountants believe that a budget variation of +- 12 cartons of golf balls per week is acceptable in sales region A. Because the budget during the third week of January was 80 cartons in region A this particular week's acceptable range of sales for the region would have been from 68 to 92 cartons (80 + 12). The Alan Company's EDP employees would have programmed their computer for this acceptable range of golf ball sales in region A.

The budget data for each week's regional golf ball sales would be contained on a computer storage medium. We will assume that the Alan Company uses magnetic tape for storing its budget data. Then, every week when the transaction tape of actual sporting goods sales is processed with the master tape containing the budget data, the computer program will check whether the actual sales of each product item fall within the acceptable limits. For golf balls, this would mean that as long as region ?A's actual third week's sales in January are within 68 to 92 cartons, no exception report on golf balls is generated. Only for those sporting goods items where the actual sales are outside the acceptable limits would an exception report be printed out for management's attention.

The type of reporting structure discussed here increases the computer's usefulness to a company's information system. The speed capability of the computer permits a timely analysis of budget versus actual sales for the individual sales personnel in their assigned regions. And, by incorporating a management-by-exception reporting structure into the company's system, the computer will print out only those significant budget variations that require management's immediate attention.

Naturally, this reporting structure can be utilized for analyzing operational performance in areas other than sales (e.g., comparing actual with standard manufacturing costs within the Alan Company's production subsystem).

The role of the accounting subsystem within an organization's operating environment is greatly influenced by top management's philosophy of organizational structure. The two major structural types are centralized and decentralized systems. When comparing centralized and decentralized organizational structures, two relevant functions should be considered : information processing and decision making.

Before computers became popular in business, many organizations were decentralized for both information processing and decision making. Under a decentralized structure, top management delegates decision-making authority and the responsibility for decisions to lower-level operating managers. Thus, before computerized data-processing systems, each subsystem was often responsible for accumulating and processing its operational data, from which the subsystem managers would make decisions (decentralized decision making).

From a behavioral viewpoint, decentralized decision making usually causes positive motivational responses by an organization's employees. People will ordinarily have higher morale and loyalty to their subsystem's goals if they have participated in making organizational decisions. Furthermore, people will often become more dedicated to their jobs if they are attempting to achieve goals they helped to establish.

The implementation of a computer into a company ordinarily centralizes the information processing functions within the electronic data processing subsystem. This may result in previous decentralized decision-making functions becoming centralized under top management.

The conversion from decentralized to centralized decision making may cause negative reactions from subsystem managers, because under decentralization these managers were directly involved in making decisions affecting their specific subsystem's operating performance. Then, upon implementing a computerized information system, each subsystem manager's previous decision making authority is removed and taken over centrally by top management.

For those organizations having computerized data-processing systems, the "ideal" organizational structure may be a integration of centralization and decentralization. The information processing functions would be centralized within the EDP subsystem. The advantages of this are to increase vastly the speed of the organization's data-processing activities and to permit more challenging work for the other subsystem's employees. The computer, in effect, takes over the often time-consuming and noncreative "busywork" of processing organizational data. For example, before a computerizsed datprocessing system existed in the Alan Company, its accountants spent large amounts of time performing bookkeeping-type functions.

With the computer taking over many of these bookkeeping activities, the accountants were able to get involved in more dynamic functions such as advising top management on financial decisions and designing more efficient and effective operating systems. The major point is that centralization of information processing does not automatically require centralization of decision making. On the contrary, centralized information processing by the

EDP subsystem will allow employees more opportunities for creative activities by eliminating much of the previous data-processing busywork from their jobs. Therefore, through computer processing of timely reports which are communicated to the specific subsystem managers requiring the report information, decentralized decision making can continue within an organization. The behavioral advantages resulting from participation by subsystem managers in decision making will also continue.

It should be emphasized, however, that even in a decentralized decision-making structure, certain organizational decisions are still typically centralized. For example, the Alan Company's top management maintains decision-making authority concerning which subsystem managers are to receive periodic salary increases as well as the specific dollar amounts of these increases.

The computer's placement within an organization is very important from a structural point of view because its location will tend to dictate the types of data processing performed. In discussing the Alan Company's system, the computer facility has been treated as a separate subsystem. However, because some organizations utilize their computers primarily for processing financial data, the EDP facility may be located within the accounting subsystem. A possible negative consequence of having the EDP facility as part of the accounting subsystem is that the accountants will exercise too much control over data-processing functions and incorporate their personal biases into the company's information system.

When computers first became popular for business data processing, they were used principally for processing financial data. This factor justified the location of the computer facility within the accounting subsystem.

However, the computer's increased popularity in business, together with the better understanding of its capabilities, has caused a large number of organizations to use their computers for nonfinancial processing activities. Marketing, for example, may use the computer for forecasting of future market demand for specific product lines.

Production managers can use the computer to help plan optimal inventory manufacturing schedules as well as to determine economic reorder points and reorder quantities for the efficient purchase of raw materials needed in the manufacturing process. Because of these varying specialized demands for computer-processed data by individual subsystems, many organizations today favor the establishment of their EDP facilities as separate subsystems.

Discussion questions

2-1. Why is it important for today's accountant to have an understanding of management concepts ?

2-2. Discuss how frustration can enter into an organization's multiplicity of goals.

2-3. What do you think is the rationale in most organizations for having strategic planning performed by top management rather than subsystem managers ?

2-4. Why is it essential for an organization's planning and controlling functions to be highly interrelated ?

2-5. Because budgets represent future financial projections and an organization's accountants are considered the financial experts, wouldn't the most expedient and efficient budgetary development approach be to have the accounting information system take complete charge for determining each subsystem's future budget? Explain.

2-6. Do you agree or disagree with the arguments given in this chapter that most organizations do not attempt to maximize their long-run profits? Discuss.

2-7. You have learned in a prior accounting course that many organizations incorporate standards for raw materials, direct labor, and production overhead into their cost accounting systems. Then, for each of these three manufacturing costs, variances are computed by comparing the actual costs with the predetermined standard costs. Let's look closer at only the raw materials manufacturing cost. Rather than computing just one total raw materials variance by comparing the actual costs with the standard costs, normally the accountant will analyze two components of the total raw materials variance: the price variance and the usage variance. What do you feel are the advantages, if any, of determining a separate price and usage variance for raw materials over computing just one total raw materials variance?

2-8. You are an accountant within the accounting information system of the Dumbo and Dang Land Development Company. Through computerized processing methods, the company's EDP subsystem handles all the financial data affecting each subsystem's operating performance. Most of the subsystem's financial data are processed weekly. Assume that you are given the job of implementing either a responsibility accounting system or a management-by-exception system into the company. Which of these two systems would you choose? Explain.

2-9. A major function of a management-by-exception reporting system is to disclose inefficient operating performance so that management can initiate corrective action. Why is it common for a management-by-exception reporting structure also to reflect favorable operating performance for which no corrective action would be necessary ?

2-10. What are some of the important ways that employees from the accounting information system and from the EDP subsystem interact in designing, implementing, and controlling a management-by-exception reporting system?

2-11. What are the major differences between a centralized organizational structure and a decentralized organizational structure? How does each of these two structures affect the role of the accounting information system in an organization?

2-12. For an organization's controlling function to be effective, why is it essential to prepare timely performance evaluation reports?

2-13. Comment on the following statement: Because an organization's computer facility will handle the processing of timely performance reports about each subsystem's operating activities, the accounting information system need no longer concern itself with the organization's performance reporting system.

2-14. Why is it important for accountants to understand the decision-making authority and responsibility of each subsystem manager in their organization ?

2-15. Because top management can delegate decision-making authority to subsystem managers, doesn't it seem logical that top management should also delegate to them the responsibility for their decisions ? Discuss.

2-16. What are the advantages, if any, to an organization of utilizing a responsibility accounting system ?

2-17. The Palmer Company has a manual data-processing system and the Pocket Company has a computerized data-processing system. Both companies are approximately the same size in terms of business volume and number of employees. For which of these two companies do you think a management-by-exception performance reporting system would be more beneficial ? Explain.

2-18. As a subsystem manager, which type of organizational structure (centralized or decentralized) would you prefer to work under ? Why ?

2-19. It was pointed out in this chapter that for an organization with a computerized data-processing system, the best organizational structure would probably be centralized information processing and decentralized decision making. Do you agree or disagree with this recommendation ? Explain.

2-20. Think of some specific organizational situations in which centralized decision making would likely be preferable to decentralized decision making.

2-21. Because accountants are not trained to be either environmental experts or psychologists, is it fair to expect them to contribute to achieving top management's nonoperational goals of pollution control and highly-motivated employees ? Explain.

2-22. The Big Bright Bagel Company began business February 15, 1988, and has established the following subsystems : accounting, electronic data processing, production of bagels, marketing and sales of bagels, and personnel. The company's top management is currently analyzing several of the important decision-making activities within its system and attempting to decide which of these decision functions should be centralized and which decentralized. The following are the activities being considered.

1. Capital expenditures for production equipment.
2. Capital expenditures for the pollution control program.
3. Establishing selling prices for the different types of bagels that are manufactured.
4. Scheduling the production of bagels.
5. Granting credit to bagel customers.
6. Allowing sales discounts to bagel customers.
7. Salary increases and promotions for subsystem managers.

Requirement

Assume that you ar hired as a consultant to help the Big Bright Bagel Company decide which of these seven decision-making functions should be centralized and which decentralized. With the limited information provided in this question, make a recommendation to the company's top management for each of these functions. Give good arguments for every recommendation.

2-23. You are a member of the Bribe Bargain Basement Company's top management. Your company currently has the following subsystems: accounting, production, marketing, and personnel. Due to the rapid growth in the past few years, the company's present manual data-processing system (under the accounting subsystem's coordination) has been unable to keep up with the increased information demands by the various subsystem's coordination) has been unable to keep up with the increased information demands by the various subsystems. Therefore, your company has decided to replace its manual data-processing system with a computerized data-processing system. As a top management executive, you are given the responsibility for deciding whether to establish the new computer facility as a separate subsystem or to integrate it within the accounting subsystem. What are some of the key factors that you should consider in reaching your decision ?

Problems

2-24. The Big Juicy Hamburger Corporation operates a chain of restaurants throughout the United States. The top management at corporate headquarters exercises control over each restaurant's following functions: the construction of each restaurant's building facility and the depreciation method selected for the building, the number of managers hired at each restaurant as well as their annual salaries, and all expenditures associated with promotional efforts and advertising at each restaurant.

The managers of the individual restaurants have decision-making authority and responsibility for all the many other operating activities associated with their specific restaurant. Presented in the following table is the monthly budget performance cost report for the Big Juicy Hamburger Corporation's restaurant (located in Springfield, Illinois) for June 1988.

Requirement

The Big Juice Hamburger Corporation's top management has decided that a responsibility accounting system would be an effective means for evaluating each restaurant's monthly operating cost performance. Prepare the June 1988 performance report for the Springfield, Illinois restaurant under the corporation's responsibility accounting system.

2-25. The Best Sellers Book Company is a publisher of college textbooks. The company's operating 'data are centrally processed by its EDP subsystem. Each subsystem receives computerized performance reports and has decision-making authority delegated from top management.

In the past few months, the managers of most subsystems have been complaining about the criteria used by top management for evaluating their operating performances. The major complaint has been the number of noncontrollable items included within an individual subsystem's performance report.

You are one of the accountants working in the company's accounting information system and have been asked by top management to design and implement a responsibility accounting system for evaluating each subsystem's monthly operating performance. You suggest to top management that a further improvement could be made in the company's performance reporting system if a management-by-exception structure were also incorporated into the new system. The top management executives agree with the suggestion, and you are given the approval to design and implement the new reporting system.

You are currently analyzing the marketing subsystem's March 1988 budget projection data compared with its actual cost performance during March under the company's old reporting system. The March 1988 performance report computer printout appeared as shown below.

After familiarizing yourself with the delegated authority given the marketing subsystem managers by top management, you accumulate the following information.

1. The marketing subsystem managers make their own decisions regarding the number of sales people and clerical people to hire as well as how much to pay these employees.
2. The marketing subsystem occupies the entire second floor of the company's building and has a separate electric utilities meter on this floor.
3. The marketing subsystem managers have complete decision-making authority for all advertising expenditures associated with promoting textbook sales.

Your next major task is to determine the variations from budget that should be considered significant. Through discussions with marketing subsystem personnel and top management, the following budget variability schedule is developed : your then talk to computer specialists within the company's EDP subsystem about the required revisions in marketing's monthly performance report. Based on the information you provided these computer specialists, they make the necessary computer program changes to accomplish your new responsibility accounting system with a management-by-exception reporting structure.

Case analyses

Dynamic Industries, a diversified manufacturer of automotive replacement parts, is a company that is growing rapidly as the result of an aggressive policy of acquisition. Board chairman John Rafferty believes that the growth of his company is sound and that the main reason for the extremely rapid growth is due to the operation of the company or a highly decentralized basis. Since growth is the result of acquiring companies that are going concerns, Rafferty encourages the managements of the subsidiary companies to carry on as they had prior to joining Dynamic Industries.

At present, discussions regarding merger are being held with Central Electronics, a company that manufactures a broad line of electronic components, many of which have applications in the defense and space industries. Central Electronics is interested in Dynamic Industries because Dynamic could supply the much-needed capital to complete the final stages of the development of a high-performance transformer and the building of a plant in which to manufacture the new product. However, George Owens, the founder and president of Central, realizes the potential dangers of merging with another company in that he might lose control of his own firm and be placed in the position of being an employee for a larger corporation.

But Rafferty continually assures Owens that Dynamic Industries operates on a highly decentralized basis and describes their concept of decentralization as follows: We expect you, as the president of a subsidiary company, to manage as you have in the past. You are successful with your own company and there is no reason why you shouldn't continue to be a success operating as a part of Dynamic.

The major functions of sales, manufacturing, engineering, and product development are all yours to do with as you see fit. In a sense we are sort of the banker; that is, we supply the money that you need for capital improvements and expansion. Even though the profits of each subsidiary company go into the corporate till, it is still like having your own company because your pay for the year is a combination of a guaranteed salary and a percentage of the net profits of your company. Thus assured, Owens decided to merge with Dynamic Industries.

During the first six months all went well and Owens saw very little of anyone from corporate headquarters. At the beginning of the seventh month, the corporate controller paid Owens a visit and explained to him in detail the company's requirements for profit planning and requested that Owens develop a profit plan, a detailed forecast of Central's revenues and operating expenses for the coming year. Though very pleasant, the controller made it quite plan that should the performance of the company devitate significantly from the forecast, a team of cost accountants and industrial engineers would arrive from headquarters to determine the cause of the deviation and to recommend necessary changes. Shortly after this experience with the controller, the industrial relations vice-president of Dynamic Industries called on Owens and informed him that a member of the corporate industrial relations staff would be on hand to conduct the coming negotiations with the union representing Central's employees.

Owens protested, saying that he had been negotiating his own labor contracts for years; however, it was explained to him that because of company-wide employee benefit plans, such as pensions and insurance, and to prevent the unions from pitting one subsidiary company against another in the area of wages, centralized control over negotiations was very necessary. At the time of this visit, the provisions of the company's salary plan were outlined to Owens and arrangements were made for the installation of the corporate clerical and supervisorhsalarh plans by a member of the headquarters industrial relations staff.

The following month Owens called Rafferty and asked what steps should be taken to secure capital for the new building intended for the manufacture of the high-performance transformer. Rafferty answered by saying, "I'll have someone from the treasurer's office call on you and show you how to fill out the forms used in requesting funds for capital expansion. It's quite a process, but remember you are only one of 15 subsidiaries and they all seem to want money at the same time. Whether or not you get it this year depends not only upon your needs but also upon the needs of the other 14 companies".

Harden Company has experienced increased production costs. The primary area of concern identified by management is direct labor. The company is considering adopting a standard cost system to help control labor and other costs. Useful historical data are not available because detailed production records have not been maintained.

Harden Company has retained Finch & Associates, an engineering consulting firm, to establish labor standards. After a complete study of the work process, the engineers recommended a labor standard of 1 unit of production every 30 minutes or 16 units per day for each worker. Finch further advised that Harden's wage rates were below the prevailing rate of $ 7 per hour. Harden's production vice-president thought this labor standard was too tight and the employees would be unable to attain it. From his experience with the labor force, he believed a labor standard of 40 minutes per unit or 12 units per day for each worker would be more reasonable. The president of Harden Company believed the standard should be set at a high level to motivate the workers, but he also recognized that the standard should be set at a level to provide adequate information for control and reasonable cost comparisons. After much discussion, management decided to use a dual standard.

The labor standard recommended by the engineering firm of one unit every 30 minutes would be employed in the plant as a motivation device, and a cost standard of 40 minutes per unit would be used in reporting. Management also concluded that the workers would not be informed of the cost standard used for reporting purposes. The production vice-president conducted several sessions prior to implementation in the plant, informing the workers of the new standard cost system and answering questions. the new standards were not related to incentive pay but were introduced at the time wages were increased to $7 per hour.

The new standard cost system was ımplemented on january 1, 1988. At the end of six months of operation, the following statistics on labour performance were presented to top management.

Raw materials quality labor mix and plant facilities and conditions have not changed to any great extent during the 6-month period.

WRT Inc

Denny Daniels is production manager of the Alumalloy Division of WRT Inc. Alumalloy has limited contact with outside customers and has no sales staff. Most of its customers are other divisions of WRT. All sales and purchases with outside customers are handled by other corporate divisions. Daniels perceives the accounting department as a historical number-generating process that provides little useful information for conducting his job. Consequently, the entire accounting process is perceived as a negative motivational device that does not reflect how hard or how effectively he works as a production manager. Daniels tried to discuss these perceptions and concerns with John Scott, the controller for the Alumalloy Division.

Scott gave Daniels little consolation. Scott stated that the accounting system and the cost reports generated by headquarters are just part of the corporate game and almost impossible for an individual to change. "Although these accounting reports are pretty much the basis for evaluating the efficiency of your division and the means corporate uses to determine whether you have done the job they want, you shouldn't worry too much. You haven't been fired yet! Besides, these cost reports have been used by WRT for the last 25 years."

Daniels perceived from taking to the production manager of the Zinc Division that most of what Scot said was probability true. However, some minor cost-reporting changes for Zinc had been agreed to by corporate headquarters. He also knew from the trade grapevine that the turnover of production managers was considered high at WRT, even through relatively few were fired. Most seemed to end up quitting, usually in disgust, because of beliefs that they were not being evaluated fairly. Typical comments of production managers who have left WRT are:

"Corporate headquarters doesn't really listen to us. All they consider are those misleading cost reports. They don't want them changed and they don't want any supplemental information."

"The accountants may be quick with numbers but they don't know anything about production. As it was, I either had to ignore the cost reports entirely or pretend they are important even though they didn't tell how good a job I had done. No matter what they say about not firing people, negative reports mean negative evaluations. I'am better off working for another company".

A recent copy of the cost report prepared by corporate headquarters for the Alumalloy Division is shown below. Daniels does not like this report because he believes it fails to reflect the division's operations properly, thereby resulting in an unfair evaluation of performance.

The Kristy Company has rown from a small operation of 50 people in 1974 to 200 employees in 1988. Kristy designs, manufactures, and sells environmental support equipment. In the early ears every item of equipment had to be designed and manufactured to meet each customer's requirements. the work was challenging and interesting for the employees as innovative techniques were often needed in the production process to complete an order according to customer's requirements. In recent years the company has been able to develop several components and a few complete units which can be used to meet the requirements of several customers.

The early special design and manufacture work has given the Kristy company a leadership position in its segment of the pollution control market. Kristy takes great pride in the superior quality of its products and this quality had contributed to its dominant role in this market segment. To help ensure high-quality performance, Kristy hires the most highly skilled personnel available and pays them above the industry average. This policy has resulted in a labor force that is very efficient, stable, and positively motivated toward company objectives.

The recent increase in government regulations requiring private companies to comply with specific environmental standards has made this market very profitable. Consequently, several competitors have entered the market segment once controlled by Kristy. While kristy still maintains a dominant position in its market, it has lost several contracts to competitors that offer similar equipment to customers at a lower price.

The Kristy manufacturing process is very labor intensive. The production employees played an important role in the early success of the company. As a result, management gave employees a great deal of freedom to schedule and manufacture customer's orders. For instance, when the company increased the number of orders accepted, more employees were hired rather than current employees being pressured to produce at a faster rate. In management's view, the intricacy of work involved required employees to have ample time to ensure the work was done right.

Management introduced a standard cost system that they believed would be beneficial to the company. they thought it would assist in identifying the most economical way to manufacture much of the equipment, would give management a more accurate picture of the costs of the equipment, and would be used in evaluating actual costs for cost control. Consequently, the company should become more price competitive. Although the introduction of standards would likely lead to some employee discontent, management was of the opinion that the overall result would beneficial. The standards were introduced on June 1, 1988.

During December, the production manager reported to the president that the new standards were creating problems in the plant. The employees had developed bad attitudes, absenteeism and turnover rates had increased, and standards were not being met. In the production manager's judgment, employee dissatisfaction has outweighed any benefits management thought would be achieved by the standard cost system. The production manager supported this contention with the data presented on the previous page for 1988, during which monthly production was at normal volume levels.

Ned Gabler has been in the shoe business for 23 years and operates Quality Footwear, a 15-store chain in New York, New Jersey, and eastern Pennsylvania. Quality Footwear has grown steadily from the first store in Manhattan to the current level. Conservative styles, quality shoes, moderate pricing, and attentiveness to customer needs have characterized the operation of Quality Footwear from the beginning.

Cabler's operations manager, Chuck Staub, keeps in touch with each of the 15 stores in the chain in order to respond to any needs or emergencies that arise and to be sure each has enough inventory on hand. There is relatively little problem in maintaining the proper assortment of shoes in stock, because each store stocks the same limited assortment of shoe styles and colors. The demands on store managers are relatively few and each manager is given latitude in running the store as long as the firm's basic policy of quality service to customers is followed. Staub's job is made easier as well by the standardization among stores in terms of limited offerings and stability in the customer base.

Quality Footwear is structured around five equal general manager levels as shown by the organizational chart. The staff is well established except for the position of general manager-facilities, which Gabler had intended to fill for the past year. Unfortunately, the acquisition of the 22 stores that make up the Twentieth Century Shoes chain has occupied most of his time. The purchase recently was finalized and has expanded Gabler's geographic sales area along the Atlantic coast into the South and South-east.

Prior to concluding an acquisition agreement, Gabler had carefully surveyed the entire organization of TCS and visited every store in the chain. The prior owners had more than doubled the number of outlets in the last three years, and Gabler believed that the haste showed by the way the stores were being operated. There were inconsistencies among stores wee being operated. There were inconsistencies among stores in terms of customer service, cleanliness and neatness, and the adequacy of shoe styles in stock. Store management seemed to vary widely from very courteous and efficient to indifferent and lackadaisical. Each store manager enjoyed a great deal of autonomy. The TCS general manager was strained to keep up with operations.

TCS serves a larger area with more stores but has lost money in two of the last three years. In addition, TCS serves a slightly different market. TCS's customers are 5 to 10 years younger and tend to be more fashi conscious; thus, the TCS market segment is more competiti and will require more promotion. TCS also carries a range of accessories that includes socks, shoelaces, polish, and some novelty items, none of which are found in the Quality stores. However, Gabler believed that the increased market area and the attractive acquisition price made up for the losses and other problems. Gabler intends to retain his conservative product line as the core of his new stores and supplement it with the best-selling lines and accessories of the TCS units in all 37 stores.

Gabler asked Satub to prepare an organizational chart that would integrate the two chains and bring the total organization to a level of profitability that Quality Footwear has experienced. Staub submitted the chart that appears.

District managers will assume responsibilities similar to those previously covered by Staub, and store managers would have the same responsibilities that had been carried by the managers of the original Quality stores. In addition, each store manager would be responsible for stocking accessories and advising central purchasing of the stock and recommending shoe lines to meet regional differences in style and demand.

Jerry Burn has just been hired as the new controller for Carinal Glassworks, Inc., a manufacturer of high-quality glassware. Burn reports directly to the vice-president of finance, John Stevenson. The controller's office consists of 15 people- the conroller and two departmental supervisors who each supervise six employees.

Stevenson was looking for a confident, able, and efficient manager to head the controllership function at Cardinal Glassworks. There was no one within the organization with the appropriate qualifications, so Stevenson had to gob outside the company. Burn met all the qualifications and also had experience as a controller with his prior employer, a computer software company. The controllership function of the computer software company was in disarray before Burn assumed the position in1980. The controller's department regained its effectiveness under Burn's leadership and contributed to making the software company financially sound. Consequently, he had a reputation for being a very intelligent, organized, and efficient manager.

Burn replaces Sad hagan, who retired after 38 years of service in various capacities with the company. Hagan was well liked by his staff. There seemed to be a relaxed atmosphere in the department because Hagan was very informal and open. He delegated responsibilities to his staff and often sought their opinions on operating matters. The staff often took their own initiative on some matters without going to Hagan first.

3

MIS: Planning and Budgeting

The organization would function on a day-to-day basis with little or no thought about future challenges and opportunities. Consequently, the organization's management may find itself at an operating disadvantage relative to those competitors who are planning their short-range and long-range futures. Both long-and short-range budgets are important to an organization's planning and controlling functions. Through a formal budgetary system, the organization attempts to quantify its long-and short-range plans so that each subsystem contributes positively to top management's goals.

Periodic performance reports comparing budget allowances with actual results inform management whether or not its goals are being achieved. Most students should already have been exposed to the procedural aspects of budgeting. Therefore, our discussion of budgetary systems will concentrate more on the valuable contribution the budget process makes to an organization's information system than on specific budget procedures.

A complete budgetary information system includes long-range budgets and short-range budgets. This objectives are threefold: (1) to examine th essential principles of a good budgetary information system, (2) to analyze the accounting information system's role in long- and short-range budgetary activities, and (3) to discuss computerized budgetary information systems.

Whether discussing long-or short-range budgeting there are three major principles that should be followed when planning and operating a budgetary system: communication, participation, and flexibility. Each of these principles will now be briefly analyzed.

Communication within budgetary system

To develop realistic budgets for the future, an organization must have information concerning its internal and external environment. The internal environment encompasses all the subsystems within the organization. Because budgetary planning covers the entire organization, each internal subsystem will be affected by the budgetary process. The external environment is a major element that affects the organization's current and future operating activities. It includes the state of the economy the degree of competition from other companies in the same industry, and the like.

The development of an effective budgetary system requires that complete information be available about each organizational subsystem. After all, how can you plan for the future without information about those subsystems that will play a role in it? In order to acquire complete information so that meaningful budgets an be developed, a communication network among the organizational subsystems must be instituted by the budget planner. This communication network cuts across all subsystems' boundaries and permits the accumulation of relevant information needed in the budget process. For example, when the Alan Company's marketing subsystem is developing the detailed product-line budget of sales for 1988, it must obtain information about such things as total market demand for sporting goods equipment and competitors' share of this market. After developing its tentative sales plan, marketing must communicate with production to ascertain whether the latter's manufacturing capacity is adequate to produce the quantity of sporting goods expected to be sold.

An organization's employees often have a negative attitude toward budgets. This is caused by the confining or restrictive nature of a budget. For example, once the budgets are established, employees are expected to operate within their budget allotments. Thus, for many people, budgets represent limitations that are imposed on them and also a means by which others "watch over" and control their performance. Consequently, there are two major reasons for having an organization's employees participate in the development of the budgetary system: (1) to motivate employees toward a positive attitude to their company's budgets and (2) to achieve more realistic budgets, thereby contributing to the company's operating performance.

If, for example, only accountants are involved in preparing the budgets, many employees working within the other subsystems may be unresponsive to their organization's budgetary system. One of the most effective means of motivating these people to react favorably to budgets is employee participation in the budgetary process. because all employees will be affected in some manner by the budgets, the organization should, within reasonable limitations, attempt to involve as many employees as possible in the budgetary planning process. A company often forms a budget committee, which is responsible for planning and controlling the company's budgets. Representatives from top management and each sub-system are included on this committee, and managerial accountants serve as committee coordinators.

The committee may also include members from the company's union to represent employee interests in such matters as equitable budget allocations for salaries and fringe benefits. Each subsystem's employees will participate in developing their departmental budget. The resulting budget then goes to the budgetary committee, which reviews the departmental requests and either accepts or rejects them.

A rejection should be accompanied by an explanation of the reasons for not approving the budget. The subsystem's employees can then go back and make the necessary changes in their original proposal. The budget committee can also make specific suggestions concerning a subsystem's dollar allotment. Once the subsystem's budget is approved by this committee and actual operating performance under the budget begins, the sub-system employees should be more positively motivated to achieve the budget because they have had a voice in determining their future course of action.

Thus, through budget participation by all organizational subsystems, the budgets can be a positive, rather than a negative, planning tool. Each subsystem's budget will reflect operational goals that its employees are motivated to accomplish. As a result, the non-operational goals of top management will likely be achieved. When developing an organization's budgets, two dangers should be avoided: (1) making the budgets too strict and (2) making them too loose.

Budgets that are "too strict" are established at such a high level of performance that very few employees are able to met them. Because employees' operating performance will be evaluated by their subsystem managers on the basis of actual results against budget projections unduly strict budgets will likely give the "appearance" of unfavorable performance. Many of the subsystems may actually be operating quite efficiently; however, with strict budgets based on the expectation of unrealistically high performance levels, they appear inefficient. This situation can cause negative employee attitudes toward the budgetary process because the employees feel they are being evaluated on unfair criteria.

Budgets that are "too loose" can also be harmful to an efficiently operated organizational system. Loose budgets are set at such a low level of performance that most employees can function inefficiently and still meet the operating targets. The inefficiencies in operating performance will not be disclosed because each subsystem will appear to be performing successfully when actual results are compared with the budget performance levels. These easily attainable budgets can cause employee lazines. Loose budgets can even be counterproductive because they do not challenge the participants and thus have the potential to make an employee feel that his or her work "does not matter."

The "ideal" budgetary system falls somewhere in between those that are too strict and those that are to loose. These budgets are often called realistic budgets because they reflect a reasonable level of performance that is neither too difficult nor too easy to achieve. In actual practice, realistic budgets are quite difficult to develop. On the one hand, operating employees will be pushing for loose budgets. At the same time, top management may be arguing for strict budgets. Consequently, for an efficient and effective budgetary system to emerge, some compromise is necessary.

One of the best techniques for achieving this compromise and the resultant realistic budgets is through subsystem employees participation in developing the budgetary plans. .PA

For example, a subsystem may initially prepare a budget projection that is too loose. When this budget is subsequently reviewed by the budget committee, however, the committee should spot the budget's looseness and make it known to the subsystem. The subsystem's management will then have to revise the budget projection to eliminate the operational looseness and make it acceptable to the committee. Thus, the participation between the subsystem's management and the budget committee in developing the budget should eventually lead to a subsystem budget that closely reflects realistic performance within the organization's system.

Although an accounting information system cannot solve the budgetary dilemma of subsystems' employees and top management, an organization's accounting information system can provide a basis for compromise. This compromise is achieved largely through periodic performance reporters identifying the causes of significant budget variations. For example, it is very difficult for a union to argue that the budgets are too strict and should therefore be loosened if the record shows that unfavorable budget performance was caused by high worker absenteeism and turnover. Similarly, it is 'very difficult for top management to argue that the prior budgets were either attainable or too loose if performance reports show that a considerable amount of overtime work from experienced employees was required to meet them. This is just common sense, yet it is equally obvious that the relevant information must be available if objective decisions are to be made regarding fair and attainable performance levels within the operating budgets. The accounting information system should be able to provide the valuable budgetary information.

The participation leading to the establishment of each subsystem's budget should be a positive motivator for budget acceptance by all the subsystems. The resultant motivation should cause the subsystems' employees to have favourable attitudes about achieving their realistic budgets. If this occurs, each subsystem will then be making a positive contribution to its organization's operating performance.

When budgets are prepared, they should reflect the best expectations of an organization's future operating activities. As the future unfolds, however, conditions may change from what was originally projected in the budgetary system. For example, a new sporting goods manufacturer may appear on the market during 1988 and greatly affect the Alan Company's original expectations of 1988 sales demand for sporting goods. When the company's budget committee was coordinating the 1988 budgets back in September 1987, it may not have been aware of this new competitor.

To achieve flexibility within a budgetary system once an organization's budgets have been prepared and actual operations commence, the budgets should be monitored continually to ascertain whether the many assumptions on which these budgets were based are still valid. If internal or external environmental factors change and make the original budget projections invalid, the budgets should be revised. This revision would take into consideration the new information about the organization's operating environment.

A flexible budgetary system should provide improved information to guide an organization's operating activities because of the most current information being incorporated into the budgets. The opposite of flexible budgets are static budgets. Once developed, static budgets are never revised, regardless of the subsequent knowledge obtained about the internal and external environment. Static budgets can result in an organization's budgetary system contributing negatively to its operations. Because additional knowledge about the organization's operating environment would not be included in its budgets under a static budgetary system, comparisons of actual operating results with budget projections could lead to improper management decision making. for example, when the Alan Company's monthly budgets of base ball sales for 1988 were originally developed in September 1987, young people's interest in playing baseball was just beginning. this factor caused the Alan Company's budget committee to underestimate the 1988 demand for baseballs. With a static budget for baseball sales, the Alan Company's managerial reports comparing 1988 actual baseball sales with 1988 budgeted baseball sales would continue to be based on the now outdated sales projections made in September 1987. .PA

Assuming that the actual week-by-week baseball sales during 1988 are continually in line with the original sales projections, the Alan Company's management would probably consider the sales activities for baseballs to be successful. This could therefore cause the company to lose the opportunity to increase its 1988 baseball sales. If flexible budgets had been utilized, the Alan Company would have revised its budgets regarding the production and sales of baseballs for the remaining months in 1988 as soon as the information about the increased market demand was known.

These production and sales revisions would have caused the company to increase its selling efforts in the baseball market. If the subsequent week-by-week actual sales did not increase, an unfavorable budget variation would occur causing management to investigate and institute corrective action.

The point of this example is that an actual operating activity may appear favorable when compared with an outdated, static budget. However, by comparing the performance of the activity with an updated, flexible budget, managerial conclusions about the activity's success may be completely different.

Flexible budgets are an important part of an organization's control system because internal and external environmental changes are immediately recognized through revised budgets. For example, a weekly computerized report comparing an organization's actual sales with its budget of sales for a newly introduced product line can provide marketing managers with timely feedback regarding consumers' reactions to this new product line. If actual weekly sales are continually below budgetary expectations, this unfavorable situation may be due to quality deficiencies in the product line. This information will permit production managers to act immediately to modify the product line's manufacturing specifications with the hope that consumer demand will subsequently increase. Based on new expectations for the revised product line, adjustments to the original sales projections will then be necessary. Because of the manufacturing specification changes, the accountants will have to provide revised cost data for the production budgetary projections associated with this product line.

Strategic planning as a long-range planning approach whereby top management establishes its organization's broad, nonoperational goals. these goals reflect the organization's "plan of attack" for long-run success. Nonoperational goals represent the framework within which each organizational subsystem develops operational goals that help to achieve these long-range goals.

In addition to their short-range operational goals for the coming year, many subsystems will be involved in long-range projects that extend beyond a one-year period. The long-range projects that re either currently in progress or being considered for future implementation form the framework of an organization's long-range budgetary system. Because an organization's long-range budgeting consists of various projects that cover a period longer than one year, another term commonly used for this type of budgeting is programming.

The relevant aspects of long-range budgeting will now be analyzed. Included in our discussion will be an example of long-range budget programs for the Alan Company.

Essential Features of Long-Range Budgeting

The essential features of an organization's long-range budgetary system are as follows.

1. A systematic method for generating program proposals by each subsystem.
2. A systematic method for evaluating program proposals, and objective criteria by which to select programs for implementation.
3. A systematic method for periodic zero-based review of ongoing programs and new program proposals.

Each of these features of a long-range budgetary system is now analyzed further.

Program proposals

Most long-range budget programs involve a major monetary expenditure tat will commit an organization to a specific course of action for several years. Therefore, each subsystem that wishes to undertake a long-range project should be required to prepare a formal proposal for the budget committee describing the project's goal its estimated costs, and its estimated benefits. It should be emphasized here, however, that normally a project will not be approved by the budget committee unless its expected benefits exceed its expected costs.

The fact that a significant long-term asset investment is associated with most program proposals makes it imperative for an organization's top management to be directly involved in reviewing the proposals and either accepting or rejecting them. Because an important function of top management is to contribute to the survival of its organization by performing long-range planning, top management's direct involvement in program proposal review is essential. The degree of top management involvement in reviewing program proposals depends on the individual company. This chapter assumes that the type of budget committee previously discussed will also be responsible for reviewing long-range program proposals and deciding whether or not to implement them.

Even though qualitative factors can influence the acceptance or rejection of a program proposal, each proposal should contain as much quantifiable data as possible. These quantifiable data should be expressed in terms of the expected dollar cash costs compared with the dollar cash benefits expected from the proposal's implementation. This provides the budget committee with a common denominator for comparing one project proposal with another, although the individual projects that are proposed may be quite dissimilar. Regardless of which subsystem is submitting a program proposal, the requirement for monetary quantification normally results in the accounting information system aiding the subsystem in gathering the monetary data.

When the four program proposals are submitted to the company's budget committee for review, the committee will be better able to compare one program with another if each program's expected monetary costs and monetary benefits are available.

Evaluating Program Proposals and Selecting Programs for Implementation

Because most organizations have only so much money annually to allocate to long-range programs, and because the total dollar cost of program proposals may exceed the maximum allocated budget expenditures, the evaluation of program proposals often results in the rejection of some projects.

The cost/benefit analysis for each program proposal

submitted to the budget committee for review should contain a comparison of the expected cash outflows with the expected cash inflows during the estimated number of future years that the program will be of value to the organization. The benefits from a program will also include any cash outflow reductions that are anticipated. For example, computerizing a company's bookkeeping procedures may cause a reduced cash outlay for clerical salaries. This expected cash savings would be one of the benefits from the proposed computer system.

The various program proposals submitted by an organization's subsystems involve future cash outflows and future cash inflows. In addition, each program's future cash flows often cover a different expected time period from those of the other program proposals: To facilitate comparison of the costs and benefits of the program proposals having different years of future value, each proposal's annual net cash flow positive net cash flow occurs when cash inflows exceed cash outflows while a negative net cash flow takes place when cash outflows exceed cash should be converted to its present value. since the Alan Company's budget committee, for example, is presently attempting to compare one project proposal with another, all project proposals should be based on the present values of their net cash flows. This will provide the committee with a comparative basis for selecting and rejecting projects.

Present value analysis is founded on the "time value of money." For example, $1 received today has more value than $1 to be received a year from today. In the former case, you have the opportunity of immediately using the dollar acquired today for some productive purpose, or, at least, putting it in a bank and collecting interest. If you must wait a full year to receive this dollar, you lose the opportunity to use it in the following 12 months.

Basically, the greater the time interval until you receive a dollar, the less valuable that dollar is today. The largest rat of return that could be earned on a dollar by having it in your possession today is called the opportunity cost. For example, if you could earn 12% annually on $1 investment, but had to wait a year to acquire the dollar, you sacrifice the opportunity to obtain the 12% return this year. Assuming you can always earn a positive return on your available cash, dollars received in the future are less valuable today.

The present value tables shown in Appendix B have been mathematically derived, based on the compounding of interest. It should be noted that both tables are based on the present value of $1. Once you know the present value of $1 for some future number of years at some opportunity cost you can convert this $1 present value result to any other present value quantity desired.

Assume, for example, that your grandfather's will specifies that you shall receive a lump-sum, payment of $5000 two years from today. If you currently had this $5000 in your possession. The present value table for a future lump-sum payment assumes that this payment does not occur until year's end. If a lump-sum payment is actually to be received at a specific time other than the end of the year, such as November 15, the present value mathematical difference would normally be minimal.

Whenever a series of equal cash flows is anticipated for several years into the future and you wish to determine the present value of these future cash flows. Present value table is used. This table assumes that each year's cash flow does not occur until the end of the year. If your opportunity cost is estimated to be 12%, the 10-year, $7000 annual net cash flow from your apartment building has a present value of $39,550. Because the present value of $1 annually for the next 10 years at an opportunity cost of 12% is $5.65, multiplying this $1 present value amount by a $7000 annual net cash flow gives you the desired answer.

Present value analysis has been covered here because it is essential for a company's budget committee to know the present value of each program proposal's anticipated costs and benefits in order to review and compare adequately all the subsystems' proposals. It should be kept in mind, however, that the actual computation of a program's present value is performed at the time the proposal is being prepared by an organizational subsystem. Because of the accountants knowledge of financial data, they will usually participate in a subsystem's cost/benefit analysis as well as the conversion of the results to present value. thus, when a subsystem submits its program proposal for budget committee review, a present value analysis has already been performed on the proposal.

After reviewing all the program proposals, the budget committee will rank each proposal based on the proposal's excess present value index. For example, the Alan Company's four program proposals submitted in September 1987 would be ranked from 1 through 4 by the budget committee. The proposal with the largest excess present value index would be ranked first, the one with the next largest excess present value index second, and so on. It should be pointed out, however, that there are other methods besides the excess present value index method for ranking program proposals. Because these methods are emphasized in other accounting courses, they will not be discussed here.

To illustrate the ranking procedure for project proposals under the excess present value index method and the resultant decision-making process by the budget committee, presents the rank hierarchy of the Alan Company's four subsystem program proposals that were submitted in September 1987.

As discloses, the key factor that determines a program proposal's ranking is the program's excess present value index. The numerator of this index reflects the total present value of the program proposal's cash benefits over its cash costs. The denominator, being the present value of the total cash asset investment, reflects the fact that for most long-range programs, dollar investments in assets are required. If a program's total cash asset investment is to be paid over a period of several years, this investment must also be converted to its present vale by using present value tables. The cash asset investments for the program proposals in are already reflected at their present values because it is assumed that the cash outlays necessary for those programs selected would be made immediately. Determining each program proposal's excess present value index provides information to the budget committee regarding how much greater the present value of a program's expected future net cash flow will be compared with the present value of the program's required cash asset investment.

If the budget committee only used each proposal's net cash flow present value as the criterion for approving or rejecting programs, and ignored its present value asset investment, mis-leading program rankings could result. For example, indicates that the Alan Company's program proposal for converting its inventory system to on-line, real-time processing has the number on ranking. Even though the new manufacturing equipment program proposal has a greater present value for its projected annual net cash flows than this proposal the former is less attractive because the present value of the asset investment required for the equipment is larger than the present value of the asset investment necessary to convert the company's inventory system to on-line, real-time processing.

The use of an excess present value index for ranking program proposals expected to contribute most productively to the efficient use of an organization's limited asset resources. By comparing the number one and the number two ranked program proposals in it can be seen that the total present value of the annual net cash flow from the inventory system proposal is 1.31 times greater than this proposal's present value asset investment, whereas the total present value of the annual net cash flow from the manufacturing equipment proposal is only 1.28 times greater than the program's present value asset investment. therefore, more efficient asset utilization is expected from the inventory system program proposal. We should point out that whenever a program proposal's excess present value index is greater than 1, the program would be expected to earn a larger rate of return than its opportunity cost. On the other hand, if the excess present value index is less than 1, the program is expected to earn a smaller rate of return than its opportunity cost. Finally, should the excess present value index be exactly equal to 1, the program would be expected to earn the same rate of return as its opportunity cost.

Assuming that the Alan Company is able to allocate maximum of $65,000 in 1988 for implementing long-range programs, the proposals ranked 1 and 2 in would be approved. the program proposals ranked 3 and 4 would have to be rejected based on the $65,000 maximum budget allocation for long-range projects. Implementing the national television promotional campaign program would cause the 1988 cost of programs to exceed the $65,000 maximum.

It should be emphasized here that the process of estimating the annual cash costs and the annual cash benefits from programs can be extremely difficult. The present values of the annual cash flows for the Alan Company's four programs were assumed to emphasize the process involved in a long-range budgetary system rather than emphasizing the detailed procedural computations required to determine each program's annual cost/benefit relationship. Which covers systems design, we will present an analysis of how a program's annual cash costs and analysis of how a program's annual cash costs and annual cash benefits are estimated. This example will illustrate the various financial analyses that must be performed on a program proposal as a basis for deciding to accept or reject the program. The specific program proposal to be examined will involved converting an organization's current manual data-processing system to a computerized system.

Two further comments are warranted regarding the data in and the budget committee's acceptance or rejection of specific program proposals. First, the risk factor associated with each program proposal was ignored. Risk refers to the possibility of the expected outcome from a proposed program not occurring. The greater the uncertainty associated with an expected outcome, the greater the risk factor. Some companies attempt to compensate for this risk factor by increasing their opportunity cost percentage on those program proposals with higher uncertainty of expected outcomes. For program proposals with less uncertainty of expected outcomes, the opportunity cost percentage can be decreased. Incorporating risk factors into program proposal analyses can have a significant effect on program rankings. It should be pointed out, however, that it is quite difficult to determine how much to increase or decrease a company's opportunity cost to include risk factors in long-range budgeting.

Second, the Alan Company accepted for implementation only those program proposals ranked 1 and 2 in because of the $65,000 maximum budget allotment in 1988 for long-range programs. Assume that the $65,000 maximum was established because this dollar amount represents the maximum cash the Alan Company can generate internally in 1988 for long-range programs. Rather than immediately reject the programs ranked 3 and 4, however, the Alan Company could investigate outside sources of cash to enable otherwise rejected programs to be accepted. As long as the anticipated rate of return from a program exceeds the cost of capital associated with external financing, raising additional cash from outside sources can be good financial strategy. The subject of outside cash sources for financing long-range programs can become quite complex; therefore, it was ignored in our analysis of the Alan Company's four program proposals.

The point should also be made here that when the estimated years of value from program proposals differ widely, it may be necessary to establish a life span that is common to all the investments being considered for implementation. To illustrate, one possible approach is to use as the time period for analysis that program proposal having the shortest estimated years of value. Program proposals with longer estimated yeas of value would be treated as if they were terminated early. The expected salvage values on the early termination date of these proposals are used to measure the proposals values as of this termination date. In the analysis of program proposals in our text, however, we will not concern ourselves with making adjustments to individual program proposals because of differing estimated years of value for various long-range project proposals.

A company;s budget committee approves specific program proposals for implementation in the coming budget year because it feels that these programs will make the greatest contributions to the organization's strategic plans. By attempting to quantify monetarily program proposals' annual cash costs and annual cash benefits, converting these costs and benefits to present values, and then comparing each program proposal's total present value of its net cash flow with the present value of the proposal's total asset investment, the budget committee has a reasonable basis for approving or rejecting specific programs. Periodic program review should be part of an organization's budgetary planning a new budget year, all of the currently operating long-range programs should be reviewed by the budget committee to ascertain whether or not the original contemplated goal of each program is actually being achieved.

Consideration should be given to dropping those programs that are not accomplishing their anticipated goals and replacing them with other, more productive long-range projects. The process of periodically reviewing both new program proposals and ongoing programs before they are approved for the subsequent year is called zero-based budgeting. The objective of zero-based budgeting is to eliminate waste and inefficiency in an organization's budgetary system. In a nutshell, zero-based budgeting prevents a company from "wasting more dollars in the future." For illustrative purposes, assume that in 1988 the Alan Company purchased only $8000 worth of the total $35,000 of new manufacturing equipment approved in the production subsystem's program.

When the budget committee is evaluating this program's achievements during the latter months of 1988 to decide whether to continue the program into 1989 the committee may believe that the increased quality level of manufactured sporting goods is not being accomplished. Rather than continue this program into 1989, thereby spending more dollars for new equipment, the budget committee may decide to drop the program and not replace the present manufacturing equipment. The new equipment already acquired during 1988 would continue to be used in the manufacturing process.

In zero-based budgeting, existing programs have no priority over new program proposals. They must compete on an equal footing for the following year's asset resources devoted to long-range programs. A cost/benefit analysis must again be performed on each existing program to ascertain whether its continuation is justified. By also performing cost/benefit analyses on all the new program proposals, priorities are re-established through a ranking hierarchy of both the existing programs and the new proposals based on their excess present value indexes, as previously discussed. The result may be that certain newly proposed programs will emerge with higher excess present value indexes than some existing programs, causing the budget committee to phase out certain old programs and replace them with the new, more efficient ones.

A zero-based budget review is quite expensive because each ongoing program has to be re-evaluated in depth. Also, the evaluation process can have adverse behavioral effects on the particular subsystems' managers whose programs are being reevaluated because no manager likes to have an ongoing program dropped. For these reasons, the zero-based review is often performed once every few years rather than annually. The hope of the budget committee is that no specific ongoing program will have a significant negative effect on the organization's strategic goals during the intervening years between zero-based reviews.

Short-range

In addition to program budgets that reflect long-range plans, an organization must also include within its budgetary information system short-range operational budgets for the coming year. Each organizational subsystem's short-range budget should reflect that subsystem's operational goals. Successful performances by the subsystems will result in their positive contributions to the goals of the total system.

Both short-range and long-range budgets are important planning and controlling devices within many organizations' information systems. Because long-range program budgets reflect an organization's plan of attack for current and future success, these budgets normally are prepared prior to the 12-month, short-term budgets. However, when planning the detailed short-term budgets, the monetary consequences of long-range approved programs must be considered.

For example, the operation of the Alan Company's long-range program that converts its inventory system from batch processing to on-line, real-time processing will begin in January 1988, and is expected to have a five-year life. During each of these five years from 1988 through 1992, when the Alan Company's short-range budgets are being planned, the costs of operating the new inventory system must be incorporated into the annual budgets. In effect, the short-range budgetary process takes the organization's long-range programs as given an attempts to ascertain annually the monetary costs and benefits of the approved programs.

Short-range budgets are often prepared according to the functional areas of an organization. Thus, the Alan Company's annual budgetary planning system would include budgets for the sales function the inventory and manufacturing functions the marketing function, the personnel function, the EDP function, and so on. Rather than emphasize the functional approach, this book will stress a more modern technique in developing an organization's short-range budgets: the responsibility center approach. A responsibility center approach to budgeting s based on the concept of a responsibility accounting system. Under this budgetary method, each subsystem's annual budget includes only those cost and/ or revenue items over which the subsystem has control.

This schematic diagram of a responsibility center is a broad representation and can be applied to most types of organizations. In a manufacturing firm, various quantities of direct raw materials, direct labor, and production overhead reflect the efforts put forth to create salable products. The specific manufacturing process represents the conversion work performed to achieve the desired outputs.

A service organization also uses combinations of inputs to obtain one or more outputs. For example, the principal input of a medical clinic is the hours of professional skill exercised by its doctors in treating patients. These hours should accomplish an intangible service product, the improvement of patients health services. Both service organizations' and not-for-profit organizations information systems will be examined intensively.

When using a responsibility center approach in developing an organization's short-range budgetary system, the various inputs must be combined somehow to arrive at a total budget allowance for the specific responsibility center involved. It is not possible, for example, to add directly 1000 units of raw materials to 400 labour-hours and arrive at any sort of common denominator to reflect the responsibility center's total short-run budgeted inputs. To arrive at a common measuring unit of a center's short-range budgeted inputs, the accounting information system will convert all of the responsibility center's dissimilar inputs to dollars of cost. The resultant total costs become a reflection of the center's resources used to achieve its specific goal.

Ideally, the outputs of a responsibility center can also be measured in dollars. For a profit-oriented organization such as a manufacturing firm or medical clinic, the output measure-ment is dollars of revenue earned from providing a product or service to the clientele. The revenue function may not always represent a complete measure of output, especially in the short run. It may be quite difficult, for example, to measure the output from an organization's promotional expenditures. The additional dollars of sales revenue resulting from an advertising promotional campaign may be impossible to quantify.

The preceding has been a general discussion to familiarize the reader with the topic of responsibility centers. It should be kept in mind that the major reason for using a responsibility center approach within an organization's budgetary system is to provide better managerial information regarding the planning and controlling of the annual budgets. Through a responsibility budgetary approach, each organizational responsibility center is held accountable for only those inputs and/or outputs it can actually cause to increase or decrease. Therefore, when actual performance varies significantly from the budget, management is able to trace this budgetary variation to the specific responsibility center accountable for the variation, and planning revisions can then began.

Since the operating characteristics of organizations often vary widely, there are several different types of responsibility centers that may be established. The four major types of responsibility centers are cost, revenue, profit, and investment centers. Based on a company's organizational design and the types of budgetary information desired, more than one of these types of responsibility centers may be incorporated into the company's system.

We will now briefly discuss each of these four approaches to establishing responsibility centers. In addition, we will examine the use of divisionalized structures within profit and investment responsibility centers.

Cost Centers

Cost centers are responsibility centers in which only inputs are measured monetarily. No attempt is made to measure a cost center's output in monetary terms. The two major types of cost centers are the engineered cost center and the discretionary cost center.

In an engineered cost center, budgetary planning and controlling are normally based on a standard cost accounting system. Utilizing financial data accumulated by the accounting information system, standard costs are determined in advance of the cost center's business performance activities. These standards represent what the center's costs should be under conditions of operating efficiency. For example, each of the Alan company's manufacturing components within its production subsystem would likely be established as a separate engineered cost center for budgetary purposes. Following the budgetary planning of each center's standard costs, the accounting information system performs budgetary control by accumulating the individual center's actual incurred costs and preparing management-by-exception reports covering significant budget variations. In the case of the alan Company, which has an EDP subsystem, the accountants will provide actual and standard cost data for each cost center to the computer facility. The company's computer then prepares these management-by-exception reports.

However, predetermined standards of efficiency cannot be developed for a discretionary cost center. By definition, discretionary costs involve the subjective judgment of management. It is extremely difficult, if not impossible, to determine an "efficient" amount of these costs for a responsibility center. Therefore, from a comparison of actual costs with budget costs within the accounting information system's report covering a discretionary costs center, no measure of efficiency can be ascertained. A good example of a discretionary cost center is the research and development component found in many organizations. This operating component is often part of a company's marketing subsystem. When, for instance, the Alan Company's budget committee is attempting to determine the dollar budgetary allowance for the research and development function, there is no way to establish a standard, efficient number of dollars for research projects. Most research projects are long term, thereby making determination of their success or failure in any 12-month time frame very difficult. Also, even though a specific research project may appear unsuccessful, some of its findings may eventually lead to other, fruitful research endeavors.

The major managerial control in a research and development discretionary cost center budget is the decisions by the budget committee regarding which research projects to undertake. Once these decisions are reached, the specific number of dollars allocated annually by the budget committee to the research and development responsibility center involves subjectivity. Subsequent accounting information system reports comparing the actual costs with the budget costs of specific projects are not designed to measure operating efficiency of the research and development function. Rather, these reports merely inform management if the actual research costs are exceeding the budget. Any requests by research personnel for additional dollar expenditures in excess of their annual budgets should require justification by these employees and formal approval by the budget committee.

Revenue centers

Revenue centers for budgetary planning and controlling are often found within the sales component of an organization's marketing subsystem. These are responsibility centers in which outputs are measured monetarily; however, no formal procedure is established for relating revenue centers monetary outputs to their monetary inputs.

Revenue center budgets are designed to measure the performance of the sales component of a company's marketing subsystem in selling products to customers. A separate revenue responsibility center should likely be maintained for each of the Alan company's product lines sold by the marketing subsystem. The revenue responsibility centers' budgets for the individual product lines are based on each products forecasted sales during the coming 12-month period. As the budget year unfolds, the Alan Company's accounting information system will accumulate the sales data for management-by-exception computer reports of actual product-line sales to budget product-line sales for every revenue center. These reports will reveal favorable and unfavorable performances by the individual revenue responsibility centers.

Even though specific managers of each revenue center are held "responsible" for meeting their budgets, the revenue budget does have limited usefulness as a tool for evaluating a center's operating efficiency. For example, the revenue center budget of the basketball sales component within the Alan company's marketing subsystem is derived by multiplying expected sales quantities of basketballs by the expected unit selling price. However, many of the relevant variables that affect the product line's actual sales quantity and actual selling price are beyond the control of the sales managers. It is therefore difficult to hold these basketball sales managers completely responsible for significant variations between actual and budgeted sales of their product line. If the company's budget committee uses the responsibility budgets for the revenue centers as its basis for evaluating specific sales managers operating performances, the committee should be aware of the many uncontrollable variables that affect the revenue centers activities. Otherwise, the budgetary information reporting system can lead to unfair evaluations of these centers' positive or negative contributions to the Alan Company's goals.

Profit centers

Under a Profit center organizational structure, a specific responsibility center is accountable for "both sides of the ledger," which are inputs and outputs. Where feasible and practical within an organization, the use of profit centers for budgetary planning and controlling has several important advantages over the use of cost centers and revenue centers. Neither cost centers nor revenue centers by themselves measure the totality of an organizational component's performance. Cost centers are responsible only for monetary inputs, with no attempt made to relate these inputs to monetary outputs. At the other extreme, revenue centers are responsible for monetary outputs, but no attempt is made to relate these outputs to monetary inputs.

For a specific organization to earn a satisfactory of net income, the efforts put forth must result in a greater amount of accomplishments. You should recognize this basic relationship between revenues and expenses as the accountant's income statement. When an organization's revenues exceed its expenses, we call profit center responsible for a specific level of income performance that will contribute positively to the company 's goals.

Another important advantage of profit centers is that the centers' manager are typically delegated more authority and responsibility for decision making, This increases the decentralization within the organization. Because the measure of performance in a profit center is broadened to included both inputs and outputs, the profit center's managers should have decision-making authority and responsibility for their inputs and outputs. To emphasize only the controllable monetary activities of a profit center when evaluating its performance, many organizations utilize a *contribution margin profit measure* for planning each center's budget. A positive contribution margin indicates that the profit center is "contributing" toward covering its noncontrollable expenses. Any excess of the contribution margin over the come for center. The profit center's operating efficiency is determined by comparing its actual contribution margin with its budgeted contribution margin.

Investment centers

In those organizations for which a significant asset investment is necessary to generate income, the *investment center* approach may be favored over the profit center approach. Both of these organizational configurations commonly use the actual contribution margin compared with the budgeted contribution margin of each responsibility center as the key criterion in evaluating operating performance. With the profit center structure, however, no direct consideration is given to the dollar investment of assets that were necessary to earn a certain level of contribution margin. Under the investment center structure, a specific responsibility center's contribution margin is directly related to the assets used while earning this contribution margin portent to all organizations, failure to relate a responsibility center's income to its investment in assets can cause misleading evaluations of the center's operating performance.

For example, assume that the home appliances department of a major manufacturer had contribution margin income of $20,000 in 1987 and #30,000 in 1988. At first glance, it may appear that the department had a significant improvement in operating performance during this two-year period. By treating the department as a profit center, top management would be evaluating the home appliances on the basis of these two earnings. Resulting in a favorable evaluation. On the other hand, if the home appliances department had been established as an investment center, the department's annual contribution margin during each of these two years would be directly related to the asset investment that was necessary to generate each years contribution margin income. On further investigation, it was determined that an $80,000 asset investment existed in the home appliances department during 1987. At the beginning of 1988, however, this department acquired $70,000 worth of additional manufacturing equipment, making its total asset investment $150,0-00 . As a result of this increased asset investment, the home appliances department's return-on-capital actually decreased from 25% in 1987 to 20% in 1988. The use of the investment center approach in evaluating the home appliances department's performance thus reveals a decline in the efficient use of assets in 1988 compared with 1987.

This illustration is oversimplified, but it serves to demonstrate the more accurate information that can be provided about a department's performance using the investment center approach. Increased contribution margin income by a department from one year to the next does not automatically reflect improved operating performance if this income growth is the result of an increased asset investment.

When an investment center's annual budget is being developed, the projected contribution margin earnings of the center should be related to its budget asset investment. In most cases, this would result in a budgeted by budgeted asset investment, a projected return-on-capital criterion can be preestablished for the investment center. The budget committee's evaluation of the investment center's operating performance would thus be based on accounting performance would thus be based on accounting information system reports comparing the center's actual return-on-capital with its budgeted return-on-capital

Divisionalization of profit and investment centers

Profit centers as well as investment centers are commonly used in large organizations having a structural configuration called *divisionalization*. Under this structural arrangement, each center is entirely responsible for the manufacturing and marketing functions relating to its product line. General Motors Corporation is a good example of a divisionalized organizational structure. Each of the corporation's automobile division is treated as a separate investment center, individually responsible for the manufacturing and marketing functions associated with its specific automobile models.

Divisionalization has both advantages and disadvantages. On the advantage side, the large degree of decision-making authority and responsibility held by the decisions' managers should motivative them more strongly to achieve their organization's goals. Also, with top management personnel at company headquarters delegating this decision-making authority and responsibility to the divisions, these higher-level managers will be relieved of the time-consuming, day-to-to operational decisions necessary at each division. Top management will thus be able to spend additional time on such important activities as strategic planning for the company's long- range future.

A disadvantage that can result from divisionalization is too much competition and friction among the division' managers. Because every division is, in effect, a separate organizational unit, it is possible for the divisions to lose sight of the fact that they are all part of one big organization. Top management at company headquarters places strong emphasis on each division's profit performance as a measure of divisional efficiency; therefore, a division's managers may become so involved in their own profitability that some of their activities actually harm other divisions' performances. This can cause overall lower accomplishments for the total organization, resulting in *suboptimization* For example, Division A of a company may have the opportunity to obtain a major manufacturing order from a customer. However, the division does not currently have machine time available within its plan to manufacture the order within the specified deadline date. Another division of the same company shortage but still might no allow Division A the temporary use of some of its idle machinery. Division A therefore loses the order, causing the division's profitability and the entire company's profitably to be less than it could have been.

To avoid a problem of this nature, the company's top management personnel must encourage cooperation among the division managers. One possible approach to achieving cooperation among divisions is for top management to give verbal praise to a specific division that aids another division's operating performance. Also, top management should encourage a "team spirit" among all its division managers and emphasize to these managers that even though certain own divisions, the activities' execution contribute positively to the organization's total goals.

Computerized budget systems

The next several sections of this chapter look at the role played by a company's EDP subsystem in the budget process. In doing so, we will discuss some ways that the computer can be used within a budgetary information system, analyze the role of quantitative methods and the computer in budget planning, examine possible responsibility center designs for the EDP subsystem, and also explain the meaning of electronic spreadsheet computer programs and briefly discuss how these programs can be utilized in an accounting information system.

Up to this point, we discussed only briefly the computer's role in the budget process. For example, in the execution of budgetary control, the computer's data-processing speed enables it to process on a timely basis management-by-exception performance reports reflecting significant budget variations. Management can thus immediately investigate these variations and initiate corrective action.

A common reaction from people with no practical experience in budgetary planning is, "Big deal! Estimating a company's future sales, planning its inventory levels to satisfy sales demands, hiring sufficient employees to handle the company's expected operating requirements, etc., all appear to be rather straightforward." Actually, quite the contrary is true. Both long- and short-range budgetary planning tend to become very complex. This complexity is caused by the many variables that must be considered when planning an organizations's budgets. The following descriptions of some of the variables that the Alan Company's budget

Committee must consider in perfo ming it budgetary functions are illustrate.

1. Historical company performance. Past historical results cannot be ignored when planning the company's future course of action because historical data often provide good insights into probable future outcomes.

2. Internal and external variables affecting sales. When forecasting future sales demand for the Alan Company's many sporting goods product lines, several key questions must be answered. For example, if an additional $20,000 is budgeted this year of advertising efforts associated with the

company's product lines, what will be the expected increase in the current year's sporting goods sales? Or, what are the adverse effects, if any, on this year's sporting goods sales as a result of increased unemployment and inflation in the economy?

3. Asset resources of company and their allocation. The Alan Company has only so many dollars' worth of asset resources such as cash and production equipment Budget decisions must be made regarding the most efficient use of these asset resources. For example, the manufacturing capacity of the company's present production equipment may be insufficient to produce the various quantities of sporting goods that the sales forecasts reveal can be sold in the coming year. A long-range decision must then be made by the budget committee either to purchase additional equipment that will enable increased sporting goods production or to maintain the present level of manufacturing equipment with the result that the production output to meet the result that the production output to meet the projected sales forecasts will be impossible. If the latter decision is made, the optimal production mix feasible based on the plant's available manufacturing capacity. This will likely result in the reduced production and the resultant lost sales of those product lines having the smallest *contribution margins*

The preceding examples demonstrate a few types of variables that must be considered in a company's budgetary planning activities. Proper consideration of these variables will normally require analyses of large volumes of data, with many of the analysis becoming quire complex. Because of the processing slowness of a manual system, its use for analyzing budget variables would require considerable time and likely slow down the entire budget-planning process. However, the availability of a computer within a company's system could greatly facilitate the analyses of many complex variables that are expected to affect a company's future financial projections.

For example, in planning the Alan Company's short-range budgets for 1988, historical financial data for the past three years should be available on a computer storage medium such as magnetic tape. Assume that the accountants on the budget committee are currently preparing projected cash flow budgets for each time internal to collect the accounts receivable from credit sales. To help the accounts in projecting these cash collections, they could request a computer report reflecting the company's collectibility experience during the past three years. The report may reveal that on the averages, for the last three years, approximately 30% of each month's credit sales is collected in the actual month, 17% in the second month following the actual sales, and the remaining 3% is written off as uncollectible.

Obtaining this information would likely be quire time-consuming under a manual data-processing system. With the use of the company's computer, however, it can be acquired rather quickly by the accountants. The credit and collection department's managers and the accountants will then discuss the historical collectibility percentages and determine whether these percentages ae reflective of the future and should thus be used in preparing the 1988 monthly cash budgets. Assuming that the decision is made to use the average collectibility percentages of the prior three years in the 1988 cash flow budgets, monthly estimations of credit sale cash collections could then be determined from multiplying the monthly projections of product-line credit sales by the collectibility percentages. These calculation would, of course, be performed by the computer, and the resultant computerized cash collection schedule would be available for subsequent use in the cash budgets. The Alan Company's computer printout budget projections of monthly ash collections from credit sales.

One of the major uses of computers in budget planning and controlling is to answer "What if" questions. For example, assume that the cash collections from credit sales data incorporated into the Alan Company's monthly cash flow budgets for 1988. Following three months of operations, a management-by-exception performance report covering the sales of baseballs reveals that actual quantity sales are far in excess of budget.

As a result, unless the baseball production level is increased, adequate inventories of this product line will not be available to met newly revised estimates of future baseball sales for the remaining months of 19888. The extra demand over budget for baseballs in analyzed by the marketing managers as a short-range condition; therefore, action to acquire additional manufacturing equipment that will increase the plant's manufacturing capacity is rejected by the budget committee. Because the plant is currently operating at near full capacity, an increase in baseball production will necessitate a reduction in the manufacture of one or more of the company's other sporting goods product lines. In reaching a budget revision decision, the budget committee will want answers to "what if" question such as the following.

1. WHAT IF, for the remaining months in 1988, we increased the production of baseball by 4000 units each month, decreased the monthly production of football by 1000 units, and decreased the monthly

production of basketballs by 2000 units? WHAT effect would this change have on future months' cash flows?

2. WHAT If we initiated the same budget revisions as in (1)? WHAT effect would this change have on future months' operating incomes?

To perform *"What if" analysis* and answer questions such as these will require considerable data-processing work. For example, in answering question 2, regarding future months' operating incomes, revised budgets for sales and revised budgets for cost of merchandise sold during each of the remaining months in 1988 will have to be prepared. Furthermore, to prepare the revised budgets for cost of merchandise sold will necessitate revised budgets for production and revised cost budgets for raw materials, direct labor, and production overhead.

Through the budget committee's use of the company's computer, however, those revised budgets that reveal the operating income performance changes from production-mix changes can be quickly prepared by the EDP subsystem. With the revised budget data in hand, the budget committee can determine whether or not to institute the inventory production revisions.

Thus, to answer "what if" question, the speed capability of a computer makes it a valuable tool for providing the budget committee with timely financial information for decisions concerning budget changes. If the financial effects from anticipated budget revisions have to be determined manually, the time interval required to provide the financial information to the budget committee will likely be so long that the committee will be unable to take immediate action on the proposed revisions. The consequences will often be reduced operating efficiency by the company due to the time delays in initiating budget revisions.

To explore further the computer's role in a budgetary information system, we will now look briefly at a few quantitative methods and their use within a computerized system for budget planning.

4

Database Management

The area of database management had began with the APOLLO project of the 1960s, which was launched in response to US President John F. Kennedy's stated goal of landing a man on the moon by the end of the decade. Since, at the time, no available systems were capable of handling the coordination of the vast amounts of data required, North American Rockwell, the prime contractor for the project, asked IBM to develop one. In response, IBM developed the Generalized Update Access Method (GUAM), which went into production in 1964. It soon became clear to IBM that this product was useful in other environments and, in 1966, the company made the product available to the general public under the name Data Language/I (DL/I). This product is really the data management component of the Information Management System (IMS), which was certainly one of the most important of the early database management systems.

In the mid-1960s a system called Integrated Data Store (I-D-S) was developed at General Electric by a team headed by Charles Bachman. This system led to a whole class of database management systems, the CODASYL systems, which are still popular and influential today.In the late 1960s, the Conference on Data Systems Languages (CODASYL), the group responsible for COBOL, tackled the problem of providing a standard for database management systems. CODASYL charged a task group, the Data Base Task Group (DBTG) with the job of developing specifications for database management systems. The DBTG did this and in 1971, CODASYL presented these specifications to the American National Standards Institute (ANSI) for adoption as a national standard. Although these specifications were not accepted as a standard by ANSI, a number of systems were developed following the CODASYL guidelines. These systems are usually called CODASYL systems or DBTG systems. In 1970, Dr. E.F. Codd presented a paper that was to have profound impact on the database community. In it, he proposed a new and, at the time, radically different approach to the management of data: the relational model.

Throughout the decade of the 1970s, the relational model was the subject of intense research activity. In addition to purely theoretical research, prototype systems were developed, the most important being a system called System R, which was developed by IBM. It was not until the 1980s, however, that commercial relational DBMS's began to appear. Systems that are at least partly relational now exist in abundance on computers ranging from the smallest micro to the largest mainframe. The 1970s and 1980s have seen the development of a number of support products to go along with DBMS's. Data dictionaries, report generators, query facilities, and non procedural languages have all been developed and, along with the DBMS, they are now a part of an entire environment, the so-called fourth generation environment. We speak of systems that contain all of these facilities as Fourth Generation Languages (4GLs) or as application generators. They represent a tremendous increase in productivity. In addition, the 1980s have seen the development of microcomputer DBMS's. As the decade has progressed, these systems have increased greatly in functionally, to the point where they rival their mainframe counterparts in a number of areas. For an excellent account of the early history of database management, see the March 1976 issue of the *ACM Computing Surveys;* in this issue, gives the history of database management and an overview of the various models; discusses the relational model; discusses the CODASYL approach; examines the hierarchical model; and presents a comparison between the relational and CODASYL approaches. There are a number of advantages to the database approach to processing, particularly when a powerful, full-functioned DBMS is used. The advantages are following.

1. Economy of scale
2. Getting more information from the same amount of data
3. Sharing of data
4. Balancing conflicting requirements
5. Enforcement of standards
6. Controlled redundancy
7. Consistency
8. Integrity
9. Security
10. Flexibility and responsiveness

11. Increased programmer productivity
12. Improved program maintenance
13. Data independence

Economy of scale

The concentration of applications in one location allows for the possibility of smaller numbers of larger and more powerful computers, which usually results in an *economy of scale*. The same economy of scale may be realized by the concentration of technical expertise. Furthermore, since many users are sharing the database, any improvement in the database will potentially benefit many different users. In general, economy of scale refers to the fact that the collective cost of several combined operations may be less than the sum of the cost of the individual operations.

Getting more information from the same smount of data

The primary goal of a computer system is to turn data into information. Even though all the data that Joan needed for a requested report was in computer files, she could not easily access it and thus could not obtain the desired information. If, however, that data were in a common database, she would be able to access it. Thus, this added *information* would now be available even though the database might not contain additional *data* not already present in the files.

Sharing of data

The data can be shared among authorized users, allowing users access to more of the data. Several users might have access to the same piece of data, e.g., a faculty member's address is changed, the change is immediately relayed to all users. In addition, new applications can be developed using the existing data in the database without the added burden of creating separate collections of files.

Balancing conflicting requirements

In order for the database approach to function adequately, there must be a person or group within the organization in charge of the database itself. This body is often called Database Administration (DBA). By keeping the overall needs of the organisation in mind, DBA can structure the database to the benefit of the entire organization, not just a single user group. While this may potentially mean that an individual user group is served less well than it might have been if it had its own isolated system, the overall organization will benefit. If the organization benefits, then, ultimately, so do the individual user groups.

Enforcement of standards

With the central control mentioned in the previous paragraph, DBA can ensure that standards for such things as data names, usages, and formats are followed uniformly throughout the organization.

Controlled redundancy

Since data that was kept separate in a file oriented system is now integrated into a single database, we no longer have multiple copies of the same data. Each of the four programmers at Marvel had his or her own FACULTY file containing, among other things, a faculty members' address. Thus the address of each faculty member appeared in at least four different places. In the database approach, since there will be only one occurrence of each faculty member, this redundancy will be eliminated. In practice, there are places where we might actually introduce some limited amount of redundancy into a database for performance reasons. But, even in these cases, we are able to keep it under tight control. This is why it is better to say that we *control* redundancy rather than *eliminate* it.

Consistency

Consistency follows from the control of elimination of redundancy. If a faculty member's address appears in only one place, there is no possibility that faculty member 111 will have the address 123 MAINST at one spot within our data and 466 WILLOW RD in another, for example.

Integrity

An integrity constraint is a rule that data in the database must follow. Here is an example of an integrity constraint: the department number given for a faculty member must be that of a department that *actually exists*.

A database has integrity of data in the database satisfies all integrity constraints that have been established. In the database approach, DBA can define validation procedures that will ensure the integrity of the database.

Security

Security is the prevention of access to the database by unauthorized users. Since DBA has control over the operational data, it can define authorization procedures to ensure that only legitimate users access the data. DBA can further allow different users to have different types of access to the same data. The payroll department at Marvel College may be able to view and change the salary of a faculty member. The insurance department may be able to view the salary of a faculty member but not change it. The speaker's bureau may not even be able to view a salary. One way DBA achieves this security is through user views. Any data items not included in the user view for a given user will not be accessible to that user. Another means of achieving security is through the use of sophisticated password schemes.

Flexibility and responsiveness

Since the data that was previously kept in several different files by several different user areas is now in the same database, it is possible to respond to request for data from multiple areas in a much easier and more flexible way. Even within a single user area, the flexibility furnished by the DBMS to locate and access data in a number of different ways aids programmers in developing new programs to satisfy user requests. The use of high-level languages allows users to do some of their own programming in a very easy way. A user who employs one such language, for example, to find all the faculty members who are assigned to department 3, who are covered by insurance plan 2, and who have salary under $20,000, need only type.

```
SELECT FACULTY_NUMBER, NAME
 FROM FACULTY
 WHERE DEPT-NUMBER   = 3 AND
 PLAN-NUMBER    = 2 AND
 SALARY < 20000
```

Employing yet another language, called a natural language, a user may actually be able to type. Give me the names and numbers of all faculty members who are in department 3, covered by plan 2 and make less than 20000. In both cases, the user can get a response to a question concerning data in the database rapidly and easily, without having to submit a request for the creation of a special program to an already overworked data processing department.

Increased programmer productivity

Since programmers accessing a database do not have to worry about the mundane data manipulation activities, as they would when accessing files, they will be more productive. Studies have shown that on the average they will be two to four times more productive; i.e., a new application can be developed in one-quarter to one-half of the time it would take if it were a straight file-oriented application. In addition, with the advent of fourth-generation languages built around database management systems, the productivity increase can be much more dramatic.

Improved program maintenance

When interacting with a DBMS, programs are relatively independent of the actual data in the database. This means that many changes to the structure of the data itself may not require maintenance to existing application programs. In a straight file environment this is not true. Even simple changes to file layouts can require substantial changes in every program that access the file. In addition, since the low-level data manipulation is handled by the DBMS, details concerning this manipulation do not appear in programs. Thus, the complexity of maintaining such logic is not a concern in a DBMS environment.

Data independence

While improving program maintenance is one important advantage of having programs independent of the structure of the database, this independence has other advantages as well. Without such independence, changes to the database structure to improve performance and to meet changing corporate requirements become very difficult. The fact that all of the programs in the system need maintenance every time a change is made to the database structure would be strong incentive not to make any of these changes. Data independence removes this obstacle to changing the structure.

Data independence occurs when the structure of the database can change without requiring the programs that access the database to change. Data independence is achieved in the database environment through the use of external views or subschemas. Each program accesses data through an external view. The underlying structure of the database would not have to change. The conceptual schema is the overall global organizational view of data. Finally the internal schema is the view of the database as seen by the computer. It is the responsibility of the DBMS to map one view to another. The only requirement imposed on the external schemas is that they can be derived from what is in the conceptual schema. Certainly, if there is no *salary* field within an external schema. If there is no relationship between customers and employees in a conceptual schema, for example, there can be no relationship between them in any external schema. The important point is that the conceptual schema could change without affecting the external schemas. Obviously, an external schema would need to be changed if some field that it required were deleted from the conceptual schema.

Similarly, an internal schema can be changed without affecting the conceptual schema. Storage details or access strategies could change, for example. Where a given field was stored as zoned decimal, we may now wish to store it as packed decimal or, perhaps, in a binary format. Where direct access to a faculty member had previously been accomplished through one scheme, say hashing, we may now wish to use another scheme, perhaps some kind of index, for this purpose.

DBA could thus make changes to the internal schema to improve the performance of the database. DBA could also make changes to the conceptual schema to respond to new requirements within the organization. In both case, the external schemas could remain the same. In this way the independence described earlier is achieved. Any decent DBMS support the external schemas of the ANSI/SPARC model. CODASYL systems call them subschemas. Many relational model systems call them views. In any case, the idea is the same: users can have their own views of what the database looks like. Likewise, any decent DBMS support, in general the conceptual and internal schemas. In this case, however, the support is often not as complete as we would like. In the ANSI/SPARC model, logical details about the structure of the database belong in the conceptual schema, and physical details about such things as the actual storage and access methods for the database belong in the internal schema. Many DBMS products do not have this clear breakdown.

Database processing

As you would expect, if there are advantages to doing something a certain way, there are also disadvantages. The database areas is no exception. There are several disadvantages regarding database processing, and they are follows.

1. Size
2. Complexity
3. Cost
4. Additional hardware requirements
5. Higher impact or a failure
6. Recovery more difficult

Size

To support all the complex functions that it must provide to users, a database management system must, by its nature, be a large program occupying megabytes of disk space as well as a substantial amount of internal memory.

Complexity

Again, the complexity and breadth of the functions furnished by a DBMS make it a complex product. Programmers and analysts must understand the features of the system in order to take full advantage of it. There is a great deal for them to learn. In addition, with many choices to make when designing and implementing a new system using a DBMS, it is possible to make these choices incorrectly, especially if the understanding of the system is not thorough enough. Unfortunately, a few incorrect choices can spell disaster for the whole project.

Cost

A good DBMS is an expensive product. By the time all the appropriate components related to the DBMS are purchased for a major mainframe system, the total price can easily into the $ 100,000 to $ 400,000 range.

Additional hardware requirements

Because of the size and complexity of a DBMS, greater hardware resources are required tan would be necessary without the DBMS. This means that if the hardware resources are not increased when a DBMS is purchased, users of the system may very well notice a severe degradation in performance.

Higher impact of a failure

Since many of the data processing resources are now concentrated in the database, a failure of any component has much more far-reaching effect than in a non database environment.

Recovery more difficult

Because of the added complexity, the process of recovering the database in the event of a catastrophe is a more complicated one, particularly if the database is being updated by a large number of users concurrently.In the early 1800's Charles Babbage, a man ahead of his time, designed the first mechanical calculating machine which had all of the components of a modern computer, including data storage areas, an output mechanism, a control unit for directing the machine's operations, and an arithmetic logic unit for performing additions at the "lightning" rate of one per second. Babbage did not call the components of his difference and analytical engines by these names of course, but his design paved the way for later development of these concepts.

Babbage's *Reflections on the Decline of Science in England and on Some of its Causes* led to the foundation of the British Association for the Advancement of Science. His concern was that science not be pursued only by the aristocracy but that it really should be a profession of those who could apply it in business and manufacturing. After 1842, Babbage's collaborator in computer design was Ada Byron, Countess of Lovelace, the daughter of the poet, Lord Byron. Ada developed the concept of programming loop and earned the reputation of the first computer programmer. Unfortunately, Ada and Babbage were frustrated in their designs because the technology was not capable of building a full-scale difference engine. Babbage's son after the turn of the 20th century, did have the machine built, and proved that it really worked unfortunately, long after cancer had claimed Ada's life at age 36.

Virtually all computers before 1950 were calculating machines. When the Electronic Numerical Integrator and Calculator was built in the early 1940's by John Mauchley and J. Presper Eckert, it could perform 3000 multiplications per second. The ENIAC contained several thousand vacuum tubes. Since the mean lifetime before failure of a vacuum tube was about 300 hours, one could expect to run the ENIAC for approximately 14 minutes before a breakdown. In those days, backup of data was already very important. The computer would be run for 10 minutes; then the contents of memory would be dumped onto a secondary storage medium, so that a relatively smooth startup could be achieved when the computer did go down. Often, hours were spent diagnosing the source of the failure before the defective tube was found and replaced.

In those early days programming a computer was a very different task from now. Rather than having the program stored in memory, the computer had to be rewired or instructions entered by switches for each program change. Though slow and ponderous, the machines still represented a tremendous breakthrough; even with hours of downtime and hours of programming, calculations were performed much more rapidly and accurately than could be done by hand.

John von Neumann is given credit for developing the concept of storing programs in the computer, along with the data, in the late 1940's. Thereafter, changing a program simply meant changing the contents of the memory locations where the program was stored. The development of codes for storing instructions and distinguishing them from data was major accomplishment of this period.

By the mid 1950's most programmers began to tire of writing their own routines for driving auxiliary memory and input/output devices each time a new program was written. For each other, they were borrowing stacks of cards which contained prewritten program to handle I/O operations. Ultimately, a number of general purpose I/O subroutines were written which could be loaded with appropriate interpreters each time a program was run. By the late 1950's FORTRAN compile-and-go routines had been composed. The programmer needed only to load program and data into the computer; the routines for compilation and I/O were already within the computer memory or readily accessible to the computer from magnetic tape or another card reader. By the early 1960's Input/Output Management Programs and routines to control the flow of jobs through the machine were built into most computers. These programs were stored as *operating Systems* on tape, drum, or disk auxiliary storage known as the "system residence" devices.

Operating systems

Operating Systems are a set of programs stored more or less permanently within the computer memory for handling tasks that have to be done for most jobs. They made it easier for programmers and began to open entirely new possibilities for using computers. Until the 1960's most computers had been run in an "open shop"; when programmers wanted to run their jobs, they signed up on the schedule for a block of time when they could use the computer. It was their responsibility to lean how to operate the computer, much as personal microcomputer owners now do.

The programmers would load whatever decks of cards they needed, including compilers and I/O handlers if necessary, into the card reader, punch the button, and wait to see what happened.

Much of their time was spent looking at lights on the console and flipping switches to correct errors. The computer was idle much of the time while the programmer/operators were trying to figure out why their programmers were not working. Often they performed a core dump, listing out the contents of primary memory, and took the listings home to study before their next turn at the machine.

It was apparent that the "open shop" was a tremendous waste of programmer talent, computer time, and money. Computers were so expensive that only the elite in science and engineering could afford them, and time was scarce. It was too expensive to buy more machines. What was to be done? Why not put programs into the Operating System to allow several jobs to be run in sequence? If one job bombs, dump the core automatically, provide the output for the programmer, and proceed to load and process the next job. This was the concept of Batching Processing. It shortened turnaround time considerably and relieved the programmer of the burden of learning how to run the computer. A new job description, that of computer operator, was created.

The next obvious step was to overlap operations. Why couldn't the Operating System handle Input/Output operations on the peripheral devices while the central processing unit was processing another program or another segment of the same program? This could further reduce equipment time, improve turnaround, and make more efficient use of the machines.

By the early 1970's operating systems had been developed which would even allow concurrent processing, two or more users on the same machine, sharing the facilities at small intervals of time. Jobs could be swapped on an *event-driven* basis; when on job ended a particular task, the status of the job could be saved, and another task could be performed. By allowing more than one job at a time on the computer, greater interchangeability of data between programs was possible, and the process of turning raw data into useful information was speeded up even more.

The next obvious step was the time sharing. Without sophisticated operating systems, stored permanently within each computer, this process was impossible. Now many users can sit at remote terminals, all believing they have complete control of the machine. Their jobs are switched in and out of the CPU at such rates, that by the time they get control after each break, only a few milliseconds have elapsed, often in time periods shorter than the persistence of vision. Time-sharing is *time-driven*; that is, each user gets a fixed block of time, usually a millisecond or two, in order.

Another major benefit of Operating Systems is that errors are reduced when the machines is under program control rather than operator control. The user's program is separated from the computer system. Either can be modified without changing the other.

The tasks performed by an operating system must include:

Job scheduling. Of all the jobs entered into the computer, whether in an event-driven environment or in a time-sharing situation, whose job gets run when? Ideally, a good operating would be able to distinguish between high and low priority jobs and also schedule tasks for the most efficient use of the CPU and peripherals. The scheduler part of a control program is responsible for these tasks.

Supervision. How is the core memory allocated to the jobs which need it? Are entire programs loaded into core at one time, or are they divided into segments or pages and an alogrithm applied to determine which pages or segments swapped out when new ones are needed? The operating system keeps track of what locations in memory are used for which tasks. The user need to be concerned about memory allocation. What if the program page swapped out happens to be the next one needed? Such a situation results in program segments being swapped in and out vigorously with no processing being done, the computer is said to be *"thrashing."* A good operating system will be capable of recognizing this situation and correcting it by choosing another swapping alogrithm, at least temporarily.

Resource allocation. If two users need the same tape drive at the same time, the operating system must be capable of allocating and deallocating, temporarily suspending operation of one program until the other releases the device. If program 1 is using Drive A and program 2 is using Drive B, what happens when program 1 requests drive B and program 2 requests drive A? Both programs would normally stop and wait for the other to release the requested drive. Such situation is called *deadlock* or "deadly embrace." The operating system must be aware of such problems and be written to avoid situations when the computer is doing nothing.

Communication with the operator and recovery from failures. An operating system must communicate with the operator, providing messages about I/O devices, machine status, which jobs are running, which tapes or disks need to be loaded or unloaded, etc. Also, should there be a failure—whether it be with the building power, a problem in memory, or of any other type—a good operating system should be able to store and then find and restart on the status at some time before failure. The operator must be given the status information and instructions by the operating system on how restart is to proceed. Ideally, data and status will be stored automatically by the operating system at short intervals so that it can be easily retrieved and updated, not just during failure but also on demand from the user.

Accounting. Most computer system require detailed statistics on who uses the machine and its peripherals for what periods of time so that appropriate billing can be done. It is a fact of life that someone must pay for the computers and their operations.

Unless a machine is entirely dedicated to one department or operation, the costs must be divided. For the computer to stop each time a new user signs on or off, so that the operator can be record the time from the clock on the wall, would not only be wasteful of computer and operator time, but also would not give a true picture of how much CPU time was used, how much peripheral time of what type was used, etc.

Operator error would be inevitably lead to arguments and problems regarding who gets charged how much.

Therefore, these functions are now usually written into the operating system. If you have used a large computer you are aware that at log off you are usually told how much time you have used.

I/O Handling. Historically, the I/O handler part of operating systems is the justification for their development. Now I/O handlers are just one part of a comprehensive system on most machines. I/O handler programs tell the computer exactly how to write or read data to or from specific peripheral devices.

Generally, each device is different, they use different data formats and have different data transfer rates, different buffer size and different methods of data transfer. Programs are stored within the operating system to handle these differences. Even if you are using a microcomputer, you will have some I/O handling operations built into the system, such as how to print onto your printer, how to write on the CRT, how to read information from the keyboard, and how to store information on and read from a disk or cassette.

The I/O handler allocates devices and auxiliary storage space to your programs and data. It control how the devices operate, organize, and close data files; maintain catalogs, and store and retrieve data. It should be noted that I/O handlers are *machine dependent*. They must be written for a specific computer and a specific peripheral attached to a machine. Also, they are not entirely self-sufficient; the user must tell the computer the parameters to be used by the data handler when information is to be transferred.

Efficiency. A perfect operating system should operate as efficiently as possible. It should be apparent that instructions for moving data from one point to another in the system are probably by far the most heavily used instructions in an operating system. These must be quickly accessed and executed. Providing status in an easily stored and retrievable form to recover from *interrupts,* whether anticipated in the form of time-driven swapping in a time sharing environment or unexpected error conditions, is critical.

Testing a newly written operating system is a difficult task at best. It is impossible to predict the uses to which the programmers will put it. Inevitably, someone wants to do something that the system was not designed to do or performs a procedure in an unexpected fashion that causes the system to fail.

Normally, because of the myriad of situations encountered that could not be anticipated by the system designer, it takes months of operation on a large machine to get the bugs out of an operating system. Also, until a system is installed at its permanent location, the designer does not know what devices the operating system should be designed to support. Everybody wants something different, and operating systems must be written as generally as possible with the realization that changes and additions will be inevitable.

Units of data

Before beginning a discussion of types of data storages and modes of computer operation, it is important to understand the basic concepts of how data is organized. All information in a digital computer is written in binary form. That is, in terms of binary digits, 0 or 1, called *bits.* A binary sequence of 8 bits is called a *byte:* e.g., 10110011 would be a byte. Normally, one byte is required to represent an alphabetic or numeric character, using one of the common codes to be discussed in the next chapter. A computer word consists of a small number of bytes.

For example, a small microcomputer may have an 8-bit word, whereas a large scientific mainframe may have as many as 8 bytes per word. The computer word is a physical concept, having reference to the computer itself and how it stores information. The word is usually the smallest amount of information that can be stored or retrieved at one time.

Logically, the way we like to see our data, a character is generally the smallest unit of data. Remember, usually a character is physically one byte long. Characters are grouped logically into fields. A field would be a string of characters representing an employee identification number, a name, etc. Fields are collected in records.

A record might contain, for example, all of the information for a given student, such as student number, year in schools, age, address, courses enrolled in, etc. A collection of records, such as all of the records for the students in a given course, would be called a data file, or simply a file.

Types of storage

Data and programs are stored in two main locations in a computer. Ideally everything would be stored in high-speed main memory within the Central Processor. This memory is called *primary memory* or core storage. Before 1970 most primary memory was made of magnetic beads or "cores" approximately one millimeter in diameter, threaded on wires. Each core was capable of holding a binary bit, 0 or 1, depending upon the direction in which it was magnetized. Core memory was bulky as well as difficult and expensive to build. Now primary memory is almost always "semiconductor" memory, integrated circuits in which, roughly speaking, a current flowing past a point represents a binary 1 and no current is a binary 0.

Semiconductor memory has advantages over core; it is much easier to build, thousands of binary bits can be packed into one small integrated circuit ship, and it is relatively cheap. Its major disadvantage is that it is "volatile"; that is, when the power goes off, no more current flows, and the memory has been lost. Core memory was permanent; a loss of current did not affect its contents. Primary memory is often still called "core" memory, even though it may not consist of magnetic cores at all.

The other location for storing data is in *auxiliary memory* Secondary memory is always a peripheral medium such as cards, magnetic tape, disks, drums, etc. Two things make auxiliary memory more attractive than primary memory for large storage capacity. First, for keeping large amounts of data, auxiliary storage media are cheaper than main memory.

More information can be stored per unit cost. Second, and perhaps more important, on machines with a small number of bits per computer word, if only one or two words are reserved for addressing, the amount of primary memory which can be directly addressed is quite small. For example, if an address is limited to 16 binary bits, then the maximum number of directly addressable memory cells is 2 = 65,536. This is the situation in many small microcomputers where the address registers are indeed two bytes long. The properties of auxiliary storage media and devices will be discussed in considerable detail through this text

Operating modes

The methods of storing and processing data can be categorized in many different ways. It is especially informative to consider the operating modes of the computer which is handling the data.

In *batch* processing mode, jobs are entered into the computer and processed one at a time sequentially. Indeed, there may be at any one time a number of different tasks waiting at the gate, for the computer to process. However, each job is completed before the next job is started. In batch mode, data is collected and sorted before being entered into the computer memory. When the data is recorded in auxiliary memory a *master* file is created; that is, the permanent file of data is recorded in sequential order. The order of the information in the file is determined by one field, called a *key*, in each record.

Updating a master file, inserting new information or deleting some records, generally requires a complete rewrite of the file. New information is collected and sorted into order by keys in a *transaction* or *detail* file. Updating is performed by a merge sort. The first records are read from the master file and from the transaction file and compared. The one which comes first is written to a new master file. Then the next records are compared, and so forth until the entire file has been rewritten. By this time a new master file has been created which contains all of the changes. The old master and transaction files are kept as *backup* at least until the next update of the file, so that information can be retrieved in case something happens to the new master file.

Assume that a master file contains record with information about types of small computers: their cost, memory size, peripherals, dealers, etc. The key by which each record is identified is the name of the company which makes the computer. The master file contains records for

1. Apre	5. Olson
2. Ather	6. Tarpen
3. Crab	7. Tinbox
4. JCN	8. Unvar

We wish to update from a transaction file which contains names of records to be added, changed, or deleted. A separate field indicates which action is to be taken. The transaction file contains

1. Brown (NEW)	3. JCN (CHANGE)
2. Homer (NEW)	4. Tinbox (DLTE)-Delete

Batch processing mode allows considerable flexibility in scheduling jobs. They can be done in priority order or in an order which can be most efficiently handled by the central processor. Resource use—of peripheral devices and human resources—can be efficiently scheduled; accounting and rerunning of jobs are facilitated. This operating made is especially useful when producing lengthy printed reports of items in key sequential order.

Multiprogramming

In 1960 IBM built a computer for the Los Alamos Scientific Laboratory which was called STRETCH. This was the first example of a multiprogramming machine. In a multiprogramming machine, two or more jobs can be run concurrently with a single central processing unit. It is important to distinguish between the words *concurrent* and *simultaneous.*

If two events happen simultaneously, they take up exactly the same place in time. Events which are happening concurrently occur at different times, but the time intervals between the events are so short that they may appear to be occurring simultaneously. On the STRETCH computer and most subsequent large machines, two or more jobs can run in the computer together, with the CPU performing the tasks alternately for each job in such short time intervals that it appears that the job are executing at the same time.

Multiprocessing

Computers periodically shut down, usually of their own volition and at the worst possible time. The occurs with such regularity that machines appear to have a diabolical nature of their own, running perfectly when routine work is being done, but inevitably shutting down when their use is most urgently needed.

This problem was much more serious in the past than now, because microminiaturization has made circuits not only smaller but more reliable. However, an urgent need has been felt and is still felt in most critical situations to provide a standby backup system. Buying two identical computers is one solution to the problem, available unfortunately only to affluent corporations or laboratories, rarely to the individual.

An alternative to having two identical computers is to have a single computer with more than one CPU, a *multiprocessing system.* If the CPU's are *symmetric,* they can be used interchangeably for doing a number of jobs. Alternatively, the CPU's can be used for doing different jobs at the same time. For example, one CPU might be controlling an I/O operation while the other is sorting data, or one might be searching a file for the desired data while the second is performing arithmetic operations. CPU's in a multiprocessing system may even by *asymmetric,* if the standby characteristics is not critical. For example, one CPU may be designed specifically to handle only I/O; all operations involving input and output are courted through that unit, allowing the other to continue its tasks without ever having to be involved in I/O operations.

Time sharing

In a time-sharing environment, whether with one or more CPU's, each user is "on-line" with the computer from a remote terminal. The time-sharer interacts directly with the computer. Processing a RETURN or ENTER key causes some action in the computer. The response is so rapid that the users feel like they are the only users of the machine. We have become spoiled, and if we have to wait more than a second for response to our requests, we complain about degradation of the response time. Programs are swapped in and out of primary memory from an auxiliary storage system as needed. Programs can be interchanged either in their entirety or in pieces, called pages or segments. In the latter case, the computer appears to have essentially unlimited core memory for programming, because the user need not worry about what pieces of a program are in the memory. It used to be that programmers had to handle program *overlays* themselves when programs were larger than the computer memory could handle all at once. Programmers had to decide how best to divide their programs up into small segments and then load and run the pieces one at a time, performing the required processing before the next overlay was loaded.

Now on a large computer an operating system does all of that. The computer is said to have *virtual memory,* as much memory as is needed to run any job. The limit to be number of users who can use a large machine at any one time is usually determined not by the size of memory but by the number of lines attaching I/O devices to the computer and by the degradation in response time which the users are willing to tolerate.

Virtual memory tends to make large computers cheaper because a smaller core is required. Data is processed as it is received, the time between runs is reduced, and computer programmers can concentrate on making their programs do the job they wish rather than on the details of how the program will run in the computer.

Another important consideration is that a large capacity direct access auxiliary storage device where tens or hundreds of megabytes are available is quite different from a tape library where hundreds of tapes are stored. With a tape library, operator intervention is constantly required to find, mount, demount, and return tapes. Errors happen often. Data is easily lost or misplaced for long periods of time. With a large capacity direct access storage device, operator intervention is minimized and data is much more secure.

Remote job entry

Closely related to the concepts of time sharing and virtual memory is the *remote job entry* operating mode. In this case, many users are connected to the machine, just as in time-sharing. However, instead of providing a response as soon as a RETURN or ENTER key is pushed at the end of each line or record, the computer generally waits until the entire job has been transmitted before it begins any program execution or data processing operations.

Direct processing

With the exception of batch sequential processing, all the modes of operation discussed above require some kind of direct processing. In direct processing mode, the data and programs can be used and stored as they are needed. It is most necessary to collect data and sort it before placing it into memory.

Access to the required data or programs is "instantaneous," or at least much more rapid than having to look at all the contents of auxiliary memory in order to retrieve the particular records desired. Direct processing has been made possible by *Direct Access Storage Devices* represented by disk and drum type auxiliary memory. You can see that direct access to data would be very difficult to achieve if that data were stored on cards or magnetic tape.

In general, direct processing mode allows more effective management of data and better controls on its security than batch mode; however, this may be at the expense of wasted space in secondary memory. As time progress, and DASD's become larger and faster, batch mode processing is being replaced more and more by direct modes of operation. Time-sharing is the accepted way of handling users on mainframe computers and on many intermediate-sized minicomputers. Even some larger microcomputers, especially those used in educational institutions, are capable of handling time-sharing, direct access mode processing.

Here are more specific examples of programming which are possible only with direct mode devices and operating systems.

1. Data files which require large amounts of storage and fast access are now feasible. For example, assume you have an inventory requirement for an automobile parts store. There are more than 8000 items in your inventory, and you need to be able not only to print out the inventory periodically but also to keep a running total of parts on hands, so that when supplies are low you can order more immediately. Thus, you can avoid having overstocks of items which tie up your capital. With direct access storage, when a part is sold or a shipment arrives, the inventory of that part can be updated immediately, without rewriting the entire inventory file. You can demand reports of items which are low in number, you can have the computer automatically warn you when an items is in short supply, and you can get your complete inventory reports when they are due.

2. We would all be very upset if we had to wait for hours for a response to a request. How many of us would visit the office of a travel agent more than once if we were told to come back tomorrow or next week to find out if our airline reservations had been

made? Virtually all airline reservations are now made on-line. A computer terminal shows flights available, a punch of a button confirms your reservation or puts you on a waiting list. Access to flight times and bookings is immediate. There is no waiting for long distance telephone calls or for a clerk to go through a file of thousands of cards or to read a magnetic tape.

3. In a bank it is impossible to predict which accounts will be active on any given day. Customer accounts must be retrievable rapidly and randomly. If there are 30,000 accounts at the bank, and the average rate of activity is 400 accounts per day, it would be absurd to have to read all accounts sequentially to find the balance for each customer who asks. In such a *low activity* situation direct access processing ideal and could not be done efficiently at all without direct access devices.

4. Suppose the management of a company wishes to expand the plant and change the way billings and payroll are handled. If that happens rarely, the files can be searched sequentially and updated by rewriting the master file. The programs can be rewritten, and the entire processing procedure can be changed. Suppose, however, you are building computers or some other high technology product, and daily changes are necessary in your programs or accounting methods. Then you want to be able to get at the exact data and the exact program segments which you wish to change, without having to change the entire package.

5. Each evening all salespersons on your force report their daily sales, what items were sold, how many, and to whom. Your records must store this

information for each salesperson, temporarily, in the order in which it is reported. Then, at the end of the pay period, the computer takes the information stored temporarily on the DASD's sorts it, updates the master payroll records, and calculates the commissions. This *intermediate storage* of information saves untold hours of processing time, which would be necessary if the information had to be sorted and processed piece by piece as it was collected.

6. Suppose you have 40 terminals in a student computer lab, and only one high-speed printer, if each student wrote directly to the printer from the computer, the system would become deadly slow, since most printers print information at a maximum rate of only a few hundred characters per second. Instead, your direct access storage device handles *spooling*. When printer output of a file is requested, the computer instead sends the data to a spool area on the DASD. The printer constantly polls the spool area to see what is there. When information is to be printed, it is read from the spool area of the DASD, not directly from the computer. Hence the computer does not have to slow down for the printer. If the spool area becomes full faster than the printer can empty it, the operating system may not allow you to write into the spool area until there is room.

The computer system

Every computer must have at least one *central processor,* where control operations and processing is actually done. Every central processor will have a *control unit,* whose job is to fetch and decode instructions and to keep track of where the next instruction is located. Also within the processor will be an *arithmetic logic* unit where calculations are performed and which directs the computer where to store results. Main or *primary memory* is also directly attached to or part of the central processing unit.

In addition, on large systems there will be *I/O channels* which run the programs necessary to drive the peripheral units. Also, one *controller* is required for each type of input or output device attached to the machine. *Auxiliary memory* storage devices, whether sequential or direct, are simply specialized input/output peripherals.

Project estimate

This is produced during the early investigation into the feasibility of a project. There will normally be several possible solutions to the problem. In order to help decide which alternative is best, we usually need to know the comparable costs.

The development cost of each possible solution must therefore be estimated. Thus, when one of the alternatives is recommended, its estimated development cost becomes the project estimate. A few points should be made about estimating.

1 It is normally done when least is known about the user's needs.

2 Nothing is known about the problems and pitfalls that will arise during the project

3 We tend to think of a straightforward solution to the problem and forget the ancillary activities of set-up, conversion, security, human inefficiency etc.

4 Subconsciously, the person making the estimate wants to please the user or their own manager and is therefore tempted to be optimistic.

5 Estimating should be based on historical data. How long has it taken us to do comparable projects in the past? What is the effective work capacity of a Team Member during a work period? Can we learn from experiences of other Project Leaders?

6 Any estimate should show a break-down of the total project into phases. A phase is a portion of the total project during which certain pre-defined tasks are carried out. This will allow us to compare each phase plan with our original estimate as the project progresses.

There are a number of surveys available on the percentage of time spent in the different phases of a project. Each company should be able to develop its own average percentages according to the type of project it undertakes and its past history of projects.

Phase plans

Depending upon the size of the project, we must plan it in a number of discrete phases. For each phase, we need two types of plan; a technical plan showing the tasks, resource and time allocation, and a financial plan which translates the resources into monetary terms. The technical plan is the main document for the Project Leader. The financial plan is the communicating document between Project Leader and Project Board. Phase plans are produced prior to the start of a phase. An exception here is the plan for the very first phase which is done as one of the first tasks of that phase.

Planning package contents

A graphic plan is inadequate alone. It needs explanation to a reader. A complete planning package should consist of:

— A graphic plan

— A description

— Assumptions on which the plan is based

— Potential problems

When our schedule slips, it will be too late to say to the contractor representative 'I thought I would have priority'. If we are making such assumptions when planning, we must make this clear to those who will approve our plan.

Resource availability plan

Before creating a technical plan for a phase, it is usually worthwhile to create a schedule showing the availability of the phase resources. This covers not only the Team Members, but also the other resources required. Such a plan will include data on when each resource becomes available, when its availability ceases, and when it is not available during the phase. The availability plan also notes holidays, training and allocation to other projects, thus providing a useful check of availability against the technical plan being created.

Deviation plan

Approval and acceptance of a phase plan means certain things. The user or customer is committed to a defined level of cost, but in turn expects the project to reach a certain point for that cost by a certain data and with a certain level of quality. If one of these factors should begin to vary beyond an agreed tolerance limit, it is the responsibility of the Project Leader to bring this to the attention of the Project Board. As described in the chapter on control, this is one at a meeting with the Project Board. At this meeting, the Project Leader will present a deviation plan. The description part of this deviation planning package describes the problem, the reason, the impact, the possible alternatives and the Project Leader's recommendation. The graphic plan will normally cover only the problem area and will extend until either the phase end or the recovery from the deviation, if this is sooner. It is not necessary for the deviation plan to go beyond the phase end. Any recovery work to be done after that will be incorporated in the next phase plan.

Planning activities

For those who like to approach planning in a methodical fashion, here is a general sequence of actions to follow. Complete the provisional 'duration' and 'end date' lines. This is achieved either by copying from the final estimate, or, if a project completion date is imposed by some external factor, by calculating the stage durations by working back from the end data.

— Remember that this is elapsed time, not manpower. Complete the resources section showing how much effort is available if the size of the Phase Team is already known.

— Examine the task checklists and mark any which are not applicable to the particular project.

— Identify any special tasks which are not in the checklists.

— Identify any necessary tasks on the checklists which have already been completed. For example, a description of the current product should normally be available.

— Consider the management of the project and allocate a percentage of manpower resource for this function throughout the plan.

— Identify, under applicable activities, those which can only be done by a certain Team Member.

— Calculate the length of time needed for each task.

— Allocate the time to produce each sub-product within the project. It is usually easiest to work backwards from the completion dates of the major tasks.

— Define which activities can be done on parallel and which must be serial

— Define quality control points

— Add to activities the time for quality control plus time for regular meetings.

— Total the resources required.

— Review the completed plan for individual workload balance, continuity of work for each Team Member, and re-cycle, where necessary, to smooth the workload.

— Determine whether any remaining time problems are best resolved by extra resources, the purchase of external products, stretching elapsed time, or reducing the facilities to be provided by the current project.

- — Calculate the cost of the planned resources.
- — Add the tolerance percentage
- — Compare with the final estimate from the feasibility study.
- — Write the plan description to provide an explanation of the graphic plan, and how it will be implemented. This description includes information on how the plan will be monitored, and the Project Leader's proposal of a suitable tolerance level.
- — List the technical and business assumptions which have been made when developing the plan. It is important to document these assumptions, so that any changes to them can be quickly identified and appropriate action taken.
- — Identify potential problems and the likely impact on the plan should they occur.

Control

Why do we need standards for the control of a project? This chapter considers the need to control various aspects of a project, and covers the control requirements of the various groups involved in a project. It is also deals with the problem of written and verbal communications in a team and project environment. The correct use of control standards enables us to answer the following questions, often asked during a project.

1. What is the quality of workmanship?
2. Are we still producing what the customer wants?
3. Are we on schedule?
4. Are we within budget?

5. Will we fail to realize that schedule or budget problems have occurred until it is too late to do anything about it?

6. How are Project Board members, not normally involved with the project on a day-to-day basis, made aware of the project status?

7. When and how often should the Project Leader meet the Project Board?

8. How do we keep control of customer requests for alterations and additional after the specification and probably the cost have been agreed? How do we prevent such requests from destroying the project schedule and budget?

Objectives

1. To pass status information upwards from Team Member to Project Board.

2. To enable the Project Leader to spot deviations from budget or schedule as soon as they occur.

3. To keep the tea informed.

4. To provide a standard procedure for meetings.

5. To identify the circumstances under which a meeting should be called.

6. To decide who should attend this meeting.

Solution

There are two major activities in control:

— Collection of project information

— Interpretation of that information to the correct people

The information is of two types:

— Technical
— Financial

In our solution, we shall consider two ways of interpreting the information and passing it on; the use of meetings and of reports. As far as our project management standards go, the collection of data will be considered from the bottom upwards. That is, gathering data from the working level and passing it upwards to Project Leader and Project Board.

The interested parties are

Project Board

Project Management Team

Project Team

Requirements

Consider the type of information each of the parties needs.

Project board

The Project Board numbers represent user and contractor management. They are not involved on a day-to-day basis. If possible, they want to manage by objectives and by exception. As management, they are mainly concerned with the status of the budget. On technical matters, they are only concerned with schedule status and knowing if the customer will get what he wants at the end of the project. They therefore do not want too much technical detail, but brief status information until things begin to go wrong. Then they need early advice of what is going wrong, together with a means of collecting all the relevant details plus technical solution proposals.

Project management team

The Project Leader needs both technical and financial information regularity. The Team Leader needs up-to-date technical progress and quality information.

Phase team

Team Members need to be able to measure their own progress against objectives, and know the status of any interfaces within the team. They need to be able to identify with the total product.

Reports

We can provide a simple recording and reporting structure to suit large and small projects. Below is a brief description of the recording and reporting activities, plus the proposed forms

Time Sheet

By: Team Members

For: Team Leader

Frequency: Daily

Team Members record efforts against tasks on time sheets.

Phase Plan

By: Team Leader

For: Project Leader

Frequency: Weekly

Effort is recorded against the phase plan from the time sheets. Completed tasks and slippages are noted.

Status report

By: Project Leader

For: Project Board

Frequency: Monthly

A brief status report is sent to the Project Board on technical status and outstanding problems.

Phase summary

By: Project Leader

For: Project Board

Frequency: Monthly

The phase summary is in graphic form to allow summarized information to be passed in a very brief document. Its main purpose is to pass financial information to the Project Board.

1 The costs of the resources consumed are recorded. A report is sent to the project Board in graphic form, comparing current phase cumulative costs and completed tasks with the plan.

2. In certain recording systems, one trap into which it is easy to fall at this time is that the team are asked to estimate 'percentage complete' for their current unfinished tasks. The danger is that this is a subjective estimate, normally optimistic, and therefore misleading. The Project Leader also has the problem of assessing all the team's estimates on different sizes of task and turning these into a single 'percentage complete' for the phase. A much better idea is the one incorporated by BP in their plan. Having produced the phase technical plan, each task in the plan is calculated as a percentage of the total phase plan. This is done by taking the total man days needed as 100% and calculating each task's effort as a percentage of that. When reporting against the plan, completed tasks are noted and their percentage totalled to give the 'percentage complete'. In reporting this figure, we ignore any tasks which have started but are not yet complete.

3 The '% Work Planned Completed' is calculated by adding up the percentages of the total phase effort of those tasks which have completed so far.

Modification requests

By: Usually a user

For: Review by the Project Board

Frequency: As required

There is one other type of report which is vital if a project is to be kept under control. There must be a document produced for every major change proposed after the feasibility study, and for every major or minor change proposed after the user specification has been signed. The implementation of such changes without proper control and authority has been responsible for many project failures to meet schedule and/or budget. Let us make this point. Having accepted the feasibility estimate, approved the user specification, and committed resources against those documents, only the Project Board has the authority to agree to any changes. Only the customer has the authority to agree to more expenditure, and this must be done at Project Board level. The procedure should be that anyone requesting a modification should document it. The request should be assessed for its impact on the project and its likely cost. All outstanding requests should be reviewed by the Project Board at the next project review meeting. Where agreement is reached to implement certain requests, the Project Board must approve the necessary extra resources and time.

Meetings

Only two types of meeting are described here; the Phase Review Meeting and the Walkthrough. The first is the formal meeting of Project Board and Team Leader at defined times during the project. The definition of these times relates to the size of the project. The second is a quality control meeting. These are the types of meeting for which must define very clear standards. There may be other types of meeting during the projects lifetime, but normally they will not require such rigorous standards.

5

Network Management

The subject of network management has become a significant part of this activity only relatively recently. It is not that the need has only just been realized. That was foreseen at the outset. Rather, the delay has been caused by the difficulty in agreeing:

OSI management standards are today and identify where further research and development is needed. To be a viable facility, network management must be as appropriate for interconnected international networks to which many businesses are attached as it is for local area networks. In this context a business may be a national or multinational enterprise operating over one or several industrial/commercial sites, it can be government, an academic or similar research community. At each site we may postulate the existence of one or more local area networks, connected to each other and to networks at remote sites as dictated by local technical needs and management policies. This scenario helps to bring out the key features of network management:

1. There are many independent management domains which have to be able to interact meaningfully yet safely.

2. There are many areas which, while not truly independent have a measure of local autonomy.

3. There will be different communication technologies involved in the networking.

4. The networks can be large and they are a strategic component of many industries.

5. The networks will evolve over time,

This chapter concerns OSI management, currently the subject of standards' activity, communications is but one of the services to be managed when information processing is distributed. Other information processing resources and activities need to be managed too, e.g. data storage, peripheral devices and processors. 'Network management' should properly include all these within its scope.

Business is dynamic. Consequently there is matching growth and decay of the networks that support the business. New requirements may lead to different types of equipment being connected to the network, or different networking technologies, with different behavioural characteristics may be introduced to meet changing workloads. As old equipment becomes obsolete and harder to maintain, it will be phased out to be replaced by newer technology. A network makes such evolution possible. Network management assists the evolutionary process and ensures that it is controllable. Management concerns the *planning, organizing, monitoring, accounting* and *control* of resources and activities. Business enterprises establish policies and provide human structures to carry out the planning and organizational activities to effect a particular management policy.

Although computers will probably be used to plan and organize, this use of information technology is usually regarded as lying outside the scope of network management. Rather, network management is more concerned with the day-to-day, operational aspects of maintaining a viable network environment; that is it is concerned with the accounting, monitoring and control functions of management. A particular aspect of management policy in many systems concerns the availability and effective use of resources. The policy may also influence the security of information and its processing in the distributed processing environment. Where the policy demands availability, it is the task of network administrators to achieve this, for example by providing duplicate resources. Where the policy also demands economy, they will find cost effective ways of providing backup. Where security is important they will ensure that the network is operated in such a manner as not to compromise user and management data.

These tasks can in principle be carried out by people, the responsiveness demanded for monitoring and the complexity of management information is such that many of the tasks are handled by the distributed information processing system itself. The network management team interacts with the processing environment to effect management policies and to provide feedback to policy makers on network behaviour. In short, network management can be implemented as an interactive, distributed processing application where the application task is that of managing the distributed processing environment. Not all parts of a large network need the same degree of management control, not all will be subject to precisely the same policies. The network environment is therefore composed of many domains of management. We define a *domain* as:

> A set of managed objects that are grouped together, for the purpose of management organization, to support a particular aspect of management.

At the outermost level, domains are determined by the boundaries of different organizations. Within organizations there can be a hierarchy of subdomains, each responsible for a given subset of resources and activities. Domains may also be established on the grounds of delegated responsibility, security, operational reporting, resource naming, etc.

Main aspects of network management

A model for network management must cover three main aspects:

- The sphere of management responsibility.
- The delegation of management responsibility.
- The objects of management concern.

The principles of management authority and responsibility require that managers exercise control within their own management domain but that they cannot exercise control outside them. Yet, to provide effective management, managers will need information about activities in other domains which may influence their own domains. They will seek to access that information and even request the delegated authority to effect controlling actions on behalf of particular distributed applications. Management responsibility may be delegated within the management domain. A management entity lying within a domain and carrying out particular management activities is termed an *agent.* These requirements lead to the following dialogue types:

- Manager to manager: to obtain information or authority for control.
- Manager to manager: to request control be exercised on a manager's behalf.
- Manager to management agent: to invoke a management operation.
- Management agent to manager: to report the occurrence of a situation.

A collaborative project in the United Kingdom to develop an advanced network system architecture has adopted a four-level hierarchy of management in which administrators respond to the directives of policy makers and effect management activities. At the base of this hierarchy are the primitive management operations. Control is exercised down the hierarchy and management information flows in the reverse direction. This simple model can be further elaborated to allow for information filtering and for feedback at intermediate levels in the hierarchy.

When a domain is distributed, the interaction between managers and agents becomes explicit. At the operations level there are no peer information flows but at higher levels there can be both peer communication and manager-to-agent communication.

At each level, control is exercised over managed objects and data values are obtained from them. Objects may be passive having values assigned to them or data read from them. Some objects may be active, i.e. changed by agencies external to management activity. Such objects may 'spontaneously' report changes in the values of their attributes to their managers.

Functional areas of management

It is generally accepted that network management covers five areas:

- Fault handling.
- Performance monitoring.
- Accounting.
- Security management.
- Configuration management.

Analysis of these areas identifies the management requirements, specific management functions and the types of managed objects involved. The following examples briefly illustrate this functional decomposition.

Fault handling is concerned with responding to situations when a system no longer meets its specification. For example, comparing a count of the successful number of transactions with a count of failed transactions will show if the error rate for a system has risen to unacceptable levels. A fault-reporting algorithm may contain a threshold to identify the level at which a fault report will be generated.

Performance monitoring records the actual behaviour of systems. For example, operations could monitor the values of the same two counters identified above to see what grade of service was being provided and if the system was meeting its management objectives. Alternatively, the rate at which transactions occur could be monitored to determine throughput.

Accounting management establishes the use that is made of the networked resources, essentially for the purpose of making a charge. Again, counters will be read that total the 'cost' of using a resource. Accounting management can also be used to exercise control over the use of resources by sanctioning only a given amount of resource to be used before warning that an accounting threshold has been reached. A further use of accounting management concerns the maintenance and communication of account records.

Because management operations influence system and network wide behaviour, it is essential that they be properly controlled. Like many other distributed applications, network management will have to demonstrate that authority exists before certain operations can be performed. The need for access control and the authentication of management actions are not of themselves aspects of network management. Rather, *security management* is the set of activities that maintain the security of the environment by controlling the way access permissions are communicated and exercised. Security management also includes activities that monitor the success with which security policies are enforced by, for example, maintaining security audit trails.

Configuration management is needed because the network and the activities within it change. As the network evolves new resources are added and old ones are discarded. The detection and rectification of faults also affects the availability of networking components. Configuration management monitors and controls the following:

- The state of resources and activities.
- The relationships between resources.
- The introduction and removal of resources,

Status is characterized both by administrative and operational attributes. Administratively a resource can be *available, unavailable* or *under test.* Operationally it may be *active* or *inactive.* Relationships characterize resource alternatives and the interconnectivity of resources. In the networking environment, configuration management controls and reports upon the path or route taken to communicate between resources. These aspects of configuration management and the need to create or delete references to both types and instances of managed objects may involve passing considerable amounts of information between systems, for example to update control tables or specify revised management algorithms.

These examples show that individual managed objects do not necessarily belong uniquely to a particular management functional area. Managed objects and their attributes, as typified by counters, gauges, reports, etc., are found in all aspects of management, and although some policy objectives may be satisfied by simple operations of the type described, many will require these simple operations to be compounded into more complex management procedures, For example, a report on the presence of a fault may lead to a check on performance. If this fell below the norm, it could lead to a change of configuration. The faulty component could be placed 'out of service' and made the subject of diagnostic tests to track down the nature of the fault in more detail.

Management standards

Users investing in distributed information technology want an open market for equipment in order to avoid being tied into a single vendor situation. They therefore welcome standardization which also brings the benefit of defined functionality and provides a yardstick against which to judge claims of conformance. These benefits of standardization apply equally to management standards though, because of the diversity of management requirement, the standards are both harder to define and to apply. Standards apply to interfaces and functions, not to the way systems are implemented. Having identified management functions, what are the interfaces? Network management is a distributed processing activity which requires a symbiosis between people and their computing systems. We identify three interfaces of concern to network management:

1. User-system.
2. System-system.
3. Application program-system.

The first two require some form of command and response language. Although the semantic requirements of such languages are similar, the syntax of the first interface is oriented towards human expression. The second interface can be optimized for efficient communication between computer systems. The third interface also concerns language but this time it is the binding between conventional programming languages and the objects of concern to management. These allow systems programmers to write programs to carry out monitoring and controlling operations. All three interfaces provide mechanisms to express the activities which a system is required to perform but, whereas the first and third are handled locally, the second interface involves the communication of the management information between systems. Thus, system-system interfaces require us to consider two aspects of standardization: (1) the end system activity and (2) the open communications between systems. The latter are expressed through open systems interconnection standards.

This distinction between the standards needed to specify the management objects and their associated operations, on the one hand, and the communication standards, on the other, is being developed in a standard document which gives an *overview* of the set of OSI management services. This standard is essentially concerned with the services to manage the OSI environment, that is the communications environment. However, research suggests that the principles it embodies are applicable to the wider aspects of management which are the subject of this chapter. An analysis of the requirements of the open communications environment shows that the OSI basic reference model has to be augmented to handle management. This extension to the reference model is specified in the OSI management framework.

The purpose of OSI management

1. It augments the protocol architecture of the OSI basic reference model by describing the principles of communication in the OSI environment when applied to communication management activities.
2. It is prescriptive of some of the management standards that will be needed.

The basic reference model encapsulates the concept of protocol exchange between peer entities at seven layers. The service provided by each layer adds value to the communication service provided by lower layers and so provides an enhanced service to a higher layer. The highest layer specifies the application specific protocol. Network management is a distributed processing application so it is not surprising that the system-system communications discussed above should be conveyed by application layer protocol exchanges. This aspect of OSI management is defined as *systems management.* However, some management information is of necessity communicated also in lower layer protocols. This may occur during failure conditions, during system boot-strap or re-configuration.

To handle these management communications, the OSI management framework defines the concept of *layer management.* It specifies the circumstances when layer management is appropriate and the constraints upon its use. For example, a network layer operating the X.25 protocol can provide accounting information relevant to a particular instance of communication as a normal part of the layer protocol. Alternatively, in a local area network that offers a broadcast facility, it is appropriate to use data link layer protocols to identify which of the attached systems is acting as manager to control the operation of the network at that level. Systems management is however specified as the norm. Whereas normal protocol exchanges ultimately serve inter-application communications, layer management exchanges are only between the systems connected at that level of protocol. However, the information being transmitted may be destined for a further system or may be transmitted as a result of a request from a distant system.

Consider the example of system A requesting system B to place a remote modem into the loop-back test mode. The communication between A and B is a systems management exchange, that between B and the modem occurs through layer management protocol. How the information is handled within system B is an implementation matter. However, the OSI management framework provides an important modelling concept, the *management information base* to cover this type of communication. The management information base is a conceptual repository of information which is accessible for management purposes.

Management information services

OSI management standards encompass the following:

- Those parts of layer protocol standards that help to maintain layer activity on behalf of all users of the layer service.
- Specifications of managed objects that are the subject of systems and layer management communications.
- A naming structure to identify managed objects.
- Abstract definitions of management information together with the specification of operations on the information.
- Procedures that may be invoked to carry out management activities.
- Operations to perform management tasks for a specific management functional area
- The definition of a common application layer service for communicating management operations between

open systems.

- A protocol specification for that communication service.
- Mappings between the definition of managed objects and their operations onto their representation in protocol exchanges.

Of these standards, those for the common management information service and protocol are the most advanced. These standards set out the rules for open communication between a manager and a management activity operating as a management agent. The standards are independent of specific management procedures and are applicable to all management functional areas. They distinguish between communications that notify managers of event reports in the agent system and operations that the manager requests of the agent. The general form of the latter is:

< operation type > < managed object identifier > < access right token > < value >

where the operation type is currently defined as one of the following:

- *Get* the value of the identified object.
- *Set* the value of the identified object.
- Perform a given *action* on the identified object.
- *Create* a managed object of a specified type.
- *Delete* the identified object.

Other operations, now being appended to the above list, are those to *cancel* a get operation and to *add* and *remove* members from a set of managed objects. The *cancel get* operation has been introduced to deal specifically with the prospect that a large amount of data may be returned to a manager who has requested a *get* operation of an agent. When network traffic is particularly heavy or the manager does not wish to be overburdened, this operation allows the original *get* to be terminated. The operation may be cancelled at any time. The protocol will ensure that the manager will know, unambiguously, whether the *get* finished normally or prematurely. Because a *get* operation leaves the agent system unchanged, there is no uncertainty concerning the state of the agent system after an early cancellation.

There are also proposals to be able to cancel *set* and *action* operations, but these are meeting with resistance because they would leave the state of the agent undefined. Although the common management information protocol is seen as the principal mechanism for the transfer of management information, there is no reason in principle why file transfer protocols should not be invoked for the transfer of very large volumes of information. All operations and notifications may require the agent system to respond to the communication to acknowledge that the operation has been performed or the notification has been dealt with. However, these standards are not concerned with the consequences of the semantics of the end system operation; these are defined by the specific management information services for each functional area and by the definitions of managed objects.

Some of the standards relating to the fault and configuration management functional areas are well advanced and draft proposals for international standards have recently been registered. One of the difficulties of standardization in this highly integrated area of OSI management standards is establishing an effective structure for the standards documents and meaningful crossreferences between standards. It would be impractical to publish the whole of OSI management as a single standard since management is a potentially open-ended activity and new aspects of the standards could be added continually. Even if a reasonable subset were to be identified, publishing all those together represents a major editorial task which would delay stable parts of the standard while the less developed parts were refined.

Two sets of documents help to maintain the coherence of this set of standards. One, the management information services overview, has already been mentioned. The other set recognizes that many objects and operations are common to several different management functions. A group of documents defines the structure of management information, the common information types, their attributes and the operations upon them, The documents provide a prescriptive method for specifying new managed object types. For each type the following information is needed:

- The individual *items* of information that can be invoked by management.
- The *permitted* operations on those items.
- The *inherent* properties of the object.
- The *implicit* relations with other information elements.
- The *specific* properties for each instance of an object type.

The documents define such objects and attributes as: status, counter, gauge, threshold, event and log. This area still needs further exploration since not only must implementations of the standard conform to the rules of the protocol exchanges but they must also conform to the definitions of the semantics of operations that take place in the end systems where management operations are performed. This presents an interesting problem since tests for conformance cannot expect common implementations of particular management operations.

Therefore, indirect methods are needed to test for conformance to a distributed management algorithm and demonstrate that the desired operations have been performed correctly. The difficulties of testing for conformance are further compounded by the nature of the management operations themselves. For example, when testing for conformance to standards related to fault reporting, it is necessary to cause a system to simulate faults to carry out the specified procedure. However, responses may be generated spuriously when the system under test is itself faulty. Also, how may one test for performance without compromising the performance one is seeking to test? Even more significantly, how does one test security management functions without compromising system security? Finally, will it be possible to check re-configuration procedures in such a way that recovery is still possible even if the implementation of the standard under test fails to conform to requirements?

OSI management standards are well aware of the above issues and that they are only scratching the surface of the possible set of management activities that may need to be expressed as standards. So far, most operations and most objects are very simple as are their mappings onto management protocol. Also, they represent only those objects of concern to the open communications environment. It is the author's contention that, in the long run, all aspects of management have to be handled in a coherent manner whether they relate to communications objects, processing resources and activities or to data storage. It will not be possible for managers to monitor and control their distributed processing environments effectively if these areas of their responsibility are handled separately.

Research into distributed systems is now sufficiently mature as to show the appropriate architectures for distributed systems. This is now being complemented by the development of standards for open distributed processing (ODP). More recent work has extended these architectural approaches to encompass management by implementing distributed systems management activities in a wide area networked test bed. As a result, there is growing confidence that the current approach to OSI management is capable of handling all aspects of management. This requires that the current standards are developed with an eye to their eventual extension. Failure to do so runs the risk of constraining the development of open distributed management standards or, worse, of developing mutually incompatible sets of standards requiring different implementation approaches. The consequences for manufacturers would be increased development cost and this would be reflected to users in the costs of products.

What then must be done to extend OSI management? Firstly, the set of objects of concern to all of management and the operations upon them must be defined. Secondly, an extended set of management procedures is needed, though these are still likely to fall within the five functional areas of management that have been established. Then the objects, their operations and the procedures have to be mapped onto the services needed to communicate the management requirement between systems. This will call for extensions to the set of common management information services and protocol. One type of extension will allow for typical control structures to be communicated, for example to express conditional constructs or to request that a set of operations be repeated. Since these constructs can be nested, the syntax of information transfer will take on some of the aspects of a block structured language.

A second type of extension will concern the conditions under which groups of activities will be performed. It will define relative priorities for remote operations and whether a group of operations shall be processed as an atomic action or whether a more relaxed processing regime is permitted. Many of these extensions will add to the functionality of the local operating system enabling its functionality to be extended over the distributed processing environment. This will assist in realizing the concept of a distributed operating system when interworking between existing systems with conventional operating systems.

This approach to the development of open distributed management is that it handles the open endedness of management requirements and the need to allow managers to manage their systems according to their own policies; that is there is HU requirement to specify a standard way in which management is performed. Drawing upon the analogy of a programming language we see that, by adopting a language structured approach to management communications with a well-defined syntax and semantics we can generate any management procedure *in a standard way* and have it communicated and interpreted *according to a standard* so that it is understood, without having to standardize the procedure itself. With such a language, procedures for remote operation can be specified for immediate action or transferred as named procedures to be invoked by a subsequent *action* primitive.

The management standards has been slow and there are, as yet, only proposed functional standards for OSI management, manufacturers have recognized the need for some management tools to handle their proprietary networking products. These provide facilities for gathering performance related data, carrying out tests and performing re-configuration of network resources. The products are largely related to managing the communications infrastructure though some local area networking products for personal computer and workstation systems do permit their users to manipulate remote processing and storage resources.

Space does not permit a full analysis of existing products. However, the current ranges of products tend not to integrate their management functions into a single package. Rather, management is performed by a loosely coordinated group of software packages. Nor is communications management coordinated with distributed processing or distributed data management. Many of the current products are concerned solely with the local area communications network on which they reside. They are frequently installed within an IBM personal computer and observe network traffic as it passes; that is on a CSMA/CD network the interface would be instructed to operate in a 'promiscuous' mode, listening to all packets on the network cable.

A similar operation is possible on token ring networks and though the packet is not processed by the management computer, it is able to monitor all traffic. Such management devices are well able to produce network traffic statistics, report packet collisions and detect ring failures. They are essentially monitoring devices. Some control can be exercised where such systems are used as filtering bridges between network segments. Also, where networks provide mechanisms for terminal multiplexing, some manufacturers offer proprietary products that restrict the services that may be accessed from a given terminal or by a given user at a terminal. In some manufacturer's offerings the different aspects of management may have to be performed from different network management devices. For example, some of the products that support the interconnection of local area networks through fibre optic cable only allow the cable environment to be managed from a special management terminal. Management of the attached local networks must be done from other terminals while management of attachments must be done from yet another control system.

These are implementation matters, for even if there is a coherent set of management standards, manu-facturers will not be obliged to place all their management functionality into one box. However, offering a coherent set of standards increases the likelihood of their doing so and, having a compatible set of management standards, allows the users to purchase networking products knowing them to be accessible, for management purposes, in a common way.

Network management has become a critical issue, especially in heterogeneous and multivendor computer networks. Also, for the success of client-server computing, effective and proper implementation of network management is essential. Client-servers with a large number of workstations need network management to manage and control the networks and the components of networks with their associated hardware and software.

Like other areas of the computer industry, network management has been undergoing rapid technological advances to meet ever increasing challenges.

It is worth mentioning that, these days, the *computer* has expanded to include desktop computers popularly known as personal computers, workstations, laptops, palm-held computers, and other computing devices, which have the intelligence to do computation and also to communicate with each other. With computer technology growing at an incredibly fast pace, it may not be proper to place limitations on what a "computer" can be. Computers can connect to one another to form a *local area network* (LAN). In LANs, there are two important computer networking scenarios. The most popular scenario is known as *client-server* computing.

In client-server computing, a client requests a service from a server and the server provides the service to the client. As an example, compiling a computer program in a client can be done by the compiler located in a server. On the other hand, in *peer-to-peer* computer networking, there are no fixed roles such as that of client or server, and any computer in the network can be a client or server. For our discussion purposes, we include both computer networking scenarios under LANs.

The evolution from hostcentric computer networks to heterogeneous LAN networks has been gradual. This transformation to LAN computing and networking is further complicated by existing applications and protocols from different standards bodies and vendors. However, the limitations of technology, protocols, and topology impose restrictions on the number of computers that can be connected to form LANs. Therefore, clusters of networks have become the trend. Once these islands of networks come into existence, the issue of connecting and managing networks becomes important. To get a better appreciation of the problems involved in the present-day network management of LANs, let us look at some of the possible LAN environments.

Some networks can be connected by *bridges* with similar LAN protocols. Here, networks A and B use similar protocols, and they are connected by bridges. Sometimes, network A and network B are known as *segments.* Here one network is using a token ring and the other network is using Ethernet. *Routers* are used to connect these networks to the backbone network. There are also cases where dissimilar networks have to be interconnected. *The gateways* are used for connecting the networks. Here one network may be using TCP/IP, and another one may be using Open Systems Interconnection (OSI) or System Network Architecture (SNA). Also, these LANs may span buildings and cities to form a *metropolitan area network* (MAN). An extension of the MAN can be found in the *wide area network* (WAN), which covers a larger area than a MAN does.

After having discussed some of the LAN scenarios, let us take some simple examples of problems involved in managing different components of a network. Suppose we have to apply a software fix to all the computers in a network. How do we do it? We cannot take a diskette and apply the fix to all the computers, especially if there are thousands of them. Or what about isolating a fault in one computer? How can we say with certainty that a problem has occurred in X computer? And we need to be sure what caused the problem, and how it can be rectified. These sets of problems assume serious proportions if computers are from different vendors. These computers may be using different software and hardware architectures. There are various ways of reporting the problems and different ways to rectify them. In some cases, these architectures may be such that the computers attached to different LANs may not communicate with each other. In some cases, it may be necessary to connect these networks to a centralized computer. How do we connect these LANs from different vendors and then manage them from a single, central point?

All of these factors make the network management of computer networks and their components, which may be widely dispersed with multivendor origins and multiprotocol operation, a highly challenging task. How we meet it is the topic of this book. Network management uses distinctions described by *open systems interconnection* (OSI) seven-layer architecture, it is imperative that we look into it right up front. The International Standards Organization (ISO) brought out the OSI architecture of seven layers for computer networking. The main idea behind partitioning computer networking functions into separate, independent subfunctions is to standardize each layer of activity more easily and expeditiously. Each layer is expected to carry out a set of functions and provide services to the layer above it.

As defined in OSI, a *system* includes computer hardware and peripherals, software, and applications, including those used for communications. *Open system* has different interpretations and connotations. We prefer the following definition: A system is said to be *open* if it supports a widely accepted and well-published set of standards. Openness is not concerned with the system technology, implementation, or how the systems are connected to one another.

The seven layers are as follows:

1. The *physical layer* deals with physical interfaces and details of the physical medium used to connect two open systems. It is concerned with mechanical, electrical, optical, functional, and procedural characteristics of the links used in data transfer.

2. The *data link layer is* responsible for reliable data transfer between two linked open systems. This may require flow control, error control and recovery, and synchronization.

3. The *network layer* provides a path for data transfer between end systems. In this layer, routing of data through a network of intermediate systems may be required. As a consequence, this layer is responsible for making connections when required, maintaining them, and terminating the connections when they are no longer needed.

4. The *transport layer* is concerned with data transfer from one end to another end. For this purpose, end-to-end error recovery and flow control may be required. Note that the network layer is concerned with data transfer from one system to another, whereas, in the transport layer, we are talking about end-to-end data transfer.

5. The *session layer* is responsible for sessions between applications. This layer also provides services for establishing, maintaining, and terminating these sessions.

6. The *presentation layer* is primarily responsible for resolving differences in the way data is represented between two applications on either end. As an example, ASCII to EBCDIC translation, or vice versa, may be done in this layer. This layer also may

provide services such as encryption and data compression.

7. The *application layer* provides services and functions required by user applications. In other words, this layer provides applications and services which are not provided by lower layers to support communication between the systems. In this layer, we may include *commitment, concurrency, and recovery (CCR).* Applications such as electronic mail and network management belong to this layer. Network management applications, which use network management, also form part of this layer.

Network management, systems management, and *enterprise management* have been variously defined. This can lead to a lot of confusion and we will therefore clearly define what these terms will mean in this book. We define *management* as monitoring and controlling the resources in computers, the resources used in the connection and communication of computers, and the applications used in the computers. There are, broadly, two models for *network management,* based on how the management activities are accomplished. This, in turn, is dependent on the computing environment. A LAN is a typical *distributed-computing environment.* Management of LAN environments can be done by peer-to-peer network management. Sometimes, this is also known as *distributed-network management.* Here managers, which undertake the network management activities, act more as peers, and there is no one central manager.

The other model is *hierarchical,* or *centralized, network manageinent. In* this model, the network management is controlled from a single point, known as a *manager.* This manager may manage network resources from a centralized computing environment. This may cover the cases where one supermanager or one centralized controlling manager may manage devices via some intermediate managers. This supermanager is also known as the *manager of manager* (MOM). All these cases are grouped under *hostcentric network management*. Some-times, this can also be termed *enterprise management.*

Definition

Many definitions are in vogue for network management. We use the one provided by IEEE Standard 802.6-1990. "Network management provides mechanisms for the monitoring, control, and coordination of all managed objects within the Physical Layer and Data Link Layer of a node." The same document also defines systems management as follows: "Systems management provides mechanisms for the monitoring, control, and coordination of all managed objects within open systems. Systems management is effected through application layer protocol." Here we have to note that *skinny stacks* or trivial upper layers can also be used. From the definitions provided by the IEEE, it is apparent that network management is a subset of the activities in systems management.

In the preceding definitions, we have to be clear on the terms *monitoring, control,* and *coordination*. This is central to the concept of systems management. Let us examine the term *monitoring* first. Resources used in computer networks have to be continuously watched, and any untoward behavior leading to the deterioration of functioning of a resource, resources, or network has to be rectified. This is more a proactive action than a reactive one. The resources have to be controlled. This means that we should be able to control how the resources behave so that they function properly. When resources have to be monitored and controlled, there is a necessary factor: coordination. If there is no coordination, the situation is a free-for-all, and chaos ensues. Not only do the activities of the managed resources have to be coordinated, but so do the facilities that monitor and control them.

Unfortunately, *systems management is* a very generic term. Readers can confuse it with management of systems used in other disciplines. This confusion is compounded by the use of different terms in the computer industry. While treating the topics of OSI and SNA, especially in the peer-to-peer arena, *systems management* is the popularly used term; thus, it is better to use this term when dealing with these protocols. In Internet, *network management* is the prevalent term; hence, this term will be used when discussing this topic. While discussing IEEE-related management of resources and layer management, we will also use the term *network management*. In other places, where it is not specifically required to make distinctions between network management and systems management, the term *network management* has been used, as well.

Goals of Network Management

Higher network availability: This involves improving the operational efficiency, which means reducing system and network downtime and improving response times. Problems in a network should be responded to as quickly as possible. In many cases, it should be possible to rectify the problems unattended. But the access and transfer of management information will require processing power and involve network traffic. Therefore, performance must be considered in the design and installation of network management.

Reduce network operational cost: Ultimately, cost reduction is one of the primary motives behind network management. Because the technology changes rapidly, management of heterogeneous systems and multiple protocols is desirable.

Reduce network bottlenecks: In some cases, network administration can be performed from a central site. Under these circumstances, it may be preferable to centrally monitor and control the activity of a network. In other cases, this activity may be distributed.

Increase flexibility of operation and integration: Networking technologies are changing at a fast rate to cater to changing requirements and needs. As new applications are used, protocols used in networking are also changing. It should be possible to absorb new technologies with the least cost. As an example, in LANs, data communication is common, but there may also be a need to integrate graphics, voice, and video capabilities as the application base expands. In addition, computer networks could be used to manage copiers and faxes.

It should be possible to add new technology and equipment without much difficulty. Also, there should not be major problems in migrating from one release of network management software to another version. Network management applications should not be overly platform-dependent for their function.

Higher efficiency: In some cases, some of the goals of network management overlap. If we reduce the network operational cost and improve the network availability, overall efficiency will increase. Here, factors such as utilization, operational cost, migration cost, and flexibility must also be considered.

Ease of use: End-user interfaces are critical for the success of any product. The use of network management applications should not involve a major learning curve. User interfaces based on object-oriented principles and technology are helpful for network management applications.

Security: Some network management functions may need security features. If some critical accounting data has to be secure, then there should be provisions for providing selective security. Here we are making the distinction between computer system and network and network management-related security. Our focus will be on the security of network management functions.

To avoid confusion with OSI layers, we have used the term *level* instead of *layer,* It may be noted that this division of functions is made to explain the concepts of overall network management systems. At the lowest level, we have the *operating system and hardware.* The operating system may be DOS, Windows NT, OS/2 Warp, Windows 95, or a combination of these. Network operating systems, such as Novell NetWare or OS/2 LAN server, are also part of this level. The resources may be on the same workstation as the operating system or they may be separate components, such as a bridge or a router. Over the operating system and hardware, we need *protocol support.* Protocol support provides distinct services; hence, it must be treated as a separate level. Protocol support includes the following:

- Layers below the application layer in OSI, UDP/IP in Internet, or layers which have similar functionality.
- Management protocols such as SNMP, CMIP, or CMOL.

- Conversion of different protocols and multiprotocols which may also be needed for supporting heterogeneous and multivendor protocols.

The level above protocol support is the *network management framework,* which provides the base for various network management applications. In the computer industry, it is becoming a trend to enable and open up this level such that different vendors and alliance partners can write network management applications. The network management framework provides for the following:

- Manager and agent functions.
- Database support such as relational databases and object-oriented databases for storing data for many network management functions and applications support. We prefer to include database support in the network management framework, because network management applications sometimes need close access to the database for topology, status, inventory of resources, logs, and other data.
- View and user interface support, which are important for the success of software applications. The base for these functions is provided in this layer.
- Network management functions, such as configuration management and fault management.

The *network management applications* area is a growing market and has the potential to produce very innovative applications. Some examples include the following:

- The business management applications area is still largely untapped. With the growing client-server market, this area has challenges and potential, especially regarding the dispersal of computing equipment and environment.

- Easy-to-use view applications can ease the tasks of system administrators. The use of multimedia and artificial intelligence has wide possibilities in this area.
- Fault identification and fault diagnostic applications such as automation applications will be in greater demand to cater to the highly decentralized nature of networks.

Performance-tuning applications are very important. Even though processor power is increasing at a rapid pace and constraints such as memory are becoming cheaper, demands on them are also increasing at a fast pace. Demands on processing power will increase as graphics, image, video, and audio applications become more prevalent.

The major emphasis is on the resources being managed, protocol support, and the network management framework. It is beyond the scope of this book to either discuss in much detail the operating system and hardware or examine in depth the network management applications area. Management of computer networks involves monitoring and controlling the different hardware, microcode, and software components of networks. Some hardware components that need to be managed are:

- *Physical media and connections:* These include physical and data link layer--related equipment. Many LAN products are coming out for these layers. The protocols used vary from IEEE 802--related products, including FDDI, frame relay, B-Integrated Services Digital Networks (BISDN), asynchronous transfer mode (ATM), Synchronous Optical Network (SONET), and other emerging protocols. Also included are products such as adapters of different protocols, concentrators, and switches.

- *Computer components:* These include storage devices, processors, printers, and others. Though Ethernet, token-ring, and token-bus adapters are considered part of the computer components, they have not been included here. We prefer to lump them under the aforementioned physical media and connections category.
- *Connectivity and interconnection components:* This refers to hardware components such as repeaters, bridges, routers, gateways, hubs, and modems.
- *Telecommunication hardware:* These are modems, multiplexers, and switches, such as, for example, an ATM switch.

Typical software to be managed includes:

- *Operating system software:* This is the bare-bones system software provided on any computer. Some examples are DOS, Windows 95, and OS/2 Warp.
- *Application software and software tools:* The application software makes computers more popular and productive. With increasing integration of video, voice, text, and imaging, applications need to be managed. As the base of multimedia applications grows, multimedia applications need to be managed, too.
- *System software in client-server computing:* Some examples are NetWare servers and OS/2 LAN servers.
- *Interconnection software:* This includes software used in repeaters, bridges, routers, gateways, and hubs. In many applications, extra functionality is provided by adding software functions on the underlying

hardware. These software applications are becoming complex, and are as important as the hardware.

- *Application software in client-server computing:* This includes the database server, file server, and print server.
- *Data communication and telecommunication software:* Management of software related to data communication and telecommunication protocols such as FDDI, ATM, and frame relay is necessary. We have specifically included this in the software section, because these protocols rely heavily on software.
- *Backbone telecommunication software:* This is increasingly used to connect different LANs. Though it is included in our earlier categories, we have added backbone telecommunication software here as well to account for the emerging backbone communication protocols.

The above mentioned wide variety of hardware and software to be managed is complicated by various protocols and differences among them. In addition, many proprietary protocols are popular and have a wide application base. Therefore, multiprotocol and multivendor products make connectivity and management daunting tasks. Broadly, the scope of network management is to manage both hardware and/or software products, which may be heterogeneous, multivendor, multiprotocol, and geographically dispersed, as well as managing the people who oversee these products.

Having introduced the topic of network management, we will examine different concepts and standards, including architectures, in the rest of the book. In some cases, to provide a better understanding and appreciation of the important concepts and methodologies involved in network management, lower-layer concepts are also briefly discussed.

LANs and WANs are becoming increasingly popular. Also, with the introduction of fiber optics, telephone tariffs are coming down. At the same time, more applications, such as voice, video, text, graphics, and images, are being added to the computing environment. Simultaneously, these applications require bandwidth beyond what we have observed in the traditional transmission of voice or data. This changing scenario is slowly bringing about the integration of data communication and telecommunications, which adds complexity to network management. The management of equipment must include switches and different components used in the telephone industry.

In addition, computing and data transmission environments are becoming increasingly heterogeneous. The different types of equipment use a variety of protocols, from standards to the proprietary ones. This adds another dimension to the management of heterogeneous, as well as multiprotocol, environments.

As one guides through the maze of protocols, standards are being advanced by vendors belonging to the telephone industry, computer industry, and government agencies. There are basically two types of standards. *De facto industry standards* become established when a target segment of the user population accepts them or when a majority of vendors uses them. In some cases, such industry standards are the result of prominent players in an industry forming cooperative bodies and introducing products that conform to the guidelines developed by these bodies.

Formal standards are mostly brought out by international, regional, or national standards bodies. In many cases, there is close cooperation among these standards bodies. Governments and their agencies, by and large, prefer formal standards. The ISO is one such body, which, as the name suggests, is an important international standards organization primarily comprising governmental agencies. At the national level, most countries have their own standards organizations. Standardization is becoming important in facilitating the compatibility of hardware and software from different vendors. From this angle, concepts of *portability, connectivity,* and *interoperability* should be emphasized. Let us examine what each term means. For portability, an application in one computer platform must be able to work with identical functions in another platform, or no modifications should be required to make an application work in different platforms.

For portability purposes, application interfaces and functions provided to interact with lower-layer software should be similar. By connectivity, we mean that a system from one vendor attaches to a similar system from a different vendor, and these systems must be able to work together. For example, two computers manufactured by different vendors must work together when connected as LANs.

Interoperability, which is closely related to connectivity, goes a step further. For interoperability, the protocols, formatting of data, and application environments must be similar, such that applications developed on two different platforms must work together. An application developed by one vendor must work with a similar application from another vendor. Let us look at an example. Electronic mail and electronic data exchange applications are quite common. For interoperability, two electronic mail systems must work together regardless of which vendors developed these systems,

Having examined some terms relevant to standardization, let us return to the topic of standards bodies. In the United States and elsewhere, computer networks connected to the Internet follow their own set of standards and have well-established procedures for bringing out standards. In addition, the Institute of Electrical and Electronics Engineers (IEEE) in the United States formulates standards for LANs and in other areas where there is a need for them. Usually, the IEEE concentrates on the standardization of lower layers such as the physical and data link layers. Most standards bodies work closely with one another and adopt each other's standards, where they are available, to avoid duplication of efforts and standards.

As software applications become more sophisticated and are developed by many vendors, there is a trend toward open systems. For open systems, conformance testing to find out whether applications really conform to the standards is becoming a norm. Many variations of standards are available; therefore, it is possible to have a set of implementations with different sets of standards at different layers. To facilitate smooth operation, some standard sets, known as *profiles,* have been developed by standards bodies. This reduces incompatibility and ensures that applications using the same profiles have interoperability.

Standards provide sufficient flexibility in implementation, which may create its own set of interoperability problems. To overcome this, many leading vendors are developing a set of profiles for network management. This effort is being pioneered by the Network Management Forum (NMF), which provides guidelines on how OSI standards must be implemented. In addition to the NMF, there are also vendor consortiums such as the Open Software Foundation (OSF), Unix International, and X/Open. Many applications are being brought out based on the work done by these groups. These consortiums also active in the network management area.

A common pitfall of standards is that they take a long time to produce. Once a problem is identified, some standards bodies take years before they bring out widely accepted standards. This presents problems in some cases. People in the industry with problems needing immediate solutions cannot wait for many years for standards to resolve these problems. Still, standards are generally useful and good for everyone in the industry. Another common complaint is that the OSI standards are too complex, and it is difficult to implement them. This may be one reason for the slow implementation of standards. Because standards bodies work on the basis of consensus, there are influences in different directions, leading to frequent changes. As a consequence, it is becoming a practice to wait for standards to stabilize and become international before implementing them.

Different Network management standards

Different network management standards are prevalent. Some are closely related to one another and, in some cases, they extend earlier protocols, taking migration aspects into consideration. Extensibility is an important part of every standard. General standards must be applicable to specialized cases and applications. In network management standards, we are interested in the following key areas:

Management functional area: This covers how network management functions are organized, how they interact with each other, and how they behave with the external components. The management functional area should also clearly delineate the scope of each network management function.

Informational area: This deals with how resources are represented from the standpoint of management actions. This has to be done in a consistent manner to facilitate smooth and easy definition of new resources. Representation of resources should also cover the scope of the management operations that can be performed on these resources. We stress the scope, because it is very important to precisely define the boundaries of these resources from the management point of view and the interactions possible with external components.

Communications area: This primarily covers management protocols. As we will notice, in network management, we use entirely different management protocols for communicating management information. The communications area should also include the communication stacks or profiles which are used to support the management protocols.

Conformance area: This is a key area for interoperability. A set of guidelines should be clearly stated for checking whether an implementation has adhered to the standards outlined. During implementation, taking too much liberty may result in incompatible implementations. This can be checked only if there are precise and clear guidelines on how implementations are to be done.

6

Understanding Internet

The telephone system is ideally suited to carry speech where a human being can concentrate on decoding the received sounds and try to understand them.In economically advanced countries a comprehensive network of telephone connections are specially designed to carry speech. This network is called the Public Switched Telephone Network (PSTN). The major problem with the PSTN is that it was designed before anyone even thought of computers.

There are a number of factors contributing to the PSTN being a poor medium for the type of signals.

i) the equipment has a frequency range of 3003400 Hz, which is not very wide for high-speed data traffic.

ii) the frequency range is not continuous; some frequencies may be used to operate equipment at exchanges, which explains how phone freaks in the USA can make calls by whistling into the telephone handset and causing the exchange to set up the call. If a data signal produces the wrong frequency the call may be disconnected.

iii) to protect the exchange equipment from damage, no DC (direct current) is allowed through the local exchange. By looking at the type of wave produced by speech against a data signal, in figure, it can be seen that the speech signal never has the same voltage continuously, whereas the data signal consists almost entirely of a continuous voltage at one of two levels. The continuous voltage is the DC part which would be removed by the exchange. Removing the DC part would seriously distort a digital data signal.

The solutions to these problems include:

1. Special equipment to convert digital data signals into audio signals which can easily be transmitted through the PSTN.
2. Private four-wire connections to the local exchange, then a fixed circuit to the remote site. This cuts out some parts of the PSTN that cause problems, but not all of them.
3. Direct links of high bandwidth most of the way between sites.
4. More recently, some PTTs now offer digital services directly to the customer, in multiples of 64K bps.

Each of these solutions represents increasing cost, but results in a higher information rate.

Solution 1—This involves the use of a MODEM (MOdulator DEModulator) on the ordinary telephone line, which converts the binary signals into audio signals and back again. Only one two-wire circuit is used, but the available bandwidth is divided to provide two channels, one in each direction. One medium — two channels.

Solution 2—When the bandwidth in solution I is insufficient, an extra two wires are added, and all the wires permanently connected. This means that some of the lost frequencies can be used.

Solution 3— Because of the way the telephone exchanges are connected together, solution 2 does not normally require special connections between exchanges. However when a high bandwidth connection is needed, say 50K bps, then some extra inter-exchange connections have to be made. If special connections are made right through, then modulation techniques may not be required.

A normal telephone handset is connected to the local exchange by two wires, which is sufficient for an electrical circuit. The subscriber can dial any other subscriber on the PSTN by passing through the local exchange. At the exchange, connections are established through a hierarchy of other exchanges. The exchanges are connected together by wideband channels which are subdivided into smaller channels; each small channel is sufficient for one call. When a call is connected the caller is allocated a series of small channels between the exchanges through to the subscriber that is being called. The subscriber can dial-up any other subscriber only by passing through the local exchange which sets up the connection. The first solution above allows a subscriber to dial-up anywhere and then transfer data by using equipment that will pass data signals through the exchange. This equipment, a slow MODEM, does not have a very high data rate: 300 bps full duplex or 600/1200 bps half duplex. To improve the data rate the local exchange has to be bypassed, but this means the dialling facility is lost. Normally British Telecom provide a four-wire connection bypassing the exchange with a small channel permanently allocated through to the destination. This through connection is called a private circuit as it can only be used by the two subscribers, one at each end. Different MODEMs can be used on private circuits to provide a faster data rate on the better bandwidth. The noise levels on a private circuit are normally lower than on a dialled connection. The third solution is used to provide a faster data rate. For this, direct connections bypassing several exchanges are made so that the required bandwidth and noise level can be obtained. All of these three methods use some of the existing telephone system. British Telecom have a special data transfer network which is designed for computer data, but uses as many of the existing methods as possible. This data network, known as PSS (Packet Switching Service).

Introduction of digital telephone exchanges will enable the provision of digital circuits direct to ordinary subscribers in the near future. The major piece of equipment needed to transfer data through the PSTN is the MODEM. Modulation is a technique that can enable information signals to be passed through a medium not really suited to them. The original, and still the major, use of modulation is in radio transmission. By using that analogy it is possible to see how modulation can be used to pass digital data signals, through a medium designed to carry voice signals.

The human voice does not travel very far on its own, and if more than one person were to try broadcasting at the same time it would be very difficult to separate out the messages. The frequency range of an original signal is called the *base band;* for the human voice a base band of 300 to 3300 Hz is used on the telephone though a wider range is possible. When two people talk at once close together, they confuse listeners because they are both using the same frequency range, the base band. To transmit speech over long distances very much higher frequencies have to be used, and care must be taken to ensure that different frequencies are used for each different transmission.

The original base band frequencies have to be increased and no two transmissions should use the same frequency range. The only problems now are how to increase the frequency of the base band signal without losing any information in the signal, and then how to recover the original signal so that the transmission can be heard in the base band. The problems are solved by modulation.

Modulation, very simply, involves superimposing the information signal on to a simple carrier signal in such a way that one, or more, components of the carrier are modified to carry the information. The technique known as 'differential phase modulation'; there are four possible phase changes (0°, 90°, 180°, 270°) so each possibility represents two bits of data. A continuous frequency simple wave is used so that only the phase component changes; figure shows the phase changes. To be able to detect the phase changes a complete wave, or cycle, is used. In any one cycle there are four possible changes that could occur, so each cycle represents two bits of information.

For instance, if we use a frequency of 1200 Hz we can have an information rate of 2400 bits per second. If a stream of zeros is transmitted, no phase change occurs during that time so the receiver and sender (modulator and demodulator) can become out of bit synchronisation. To overcome this an alternative differential, phase modulation encoding scheme is used on newer MODEMs. Notice that every code now has a phase change from the previous cycle, enabling the bit synchronisation to be maintained.

The MODEM

This section describes three MODEMs to illustrate the practical arrangements made to use the PSTN for binary data using the modulation techniques previously described. The frequencies mentioned are standard CCITT recommendations; they are not the same as those used on some MODEMs in the US.

A Timesharing Terminal MODEM

A timesharing terminal is restricted by the typing and reading speed of a human being, and as such it has a relatively low data rate. The terminal also needs a full duplex connection. The MODEM used to provide the timesharing terminal with a connection to a remote computer divides the bandwidth on the PSTN into two parts to provide two channels. Normally this MODEM is connected to an ordinary telephone line, allowing the user to dial any computer he wishes, but of course this means passing through the local exchange using a two-wire circuit. The timesharing MODEM uses frequency shift keying to implement the two channels; the frequencies are

Channel 1	binary 0	1180 Hz
	binary 1	980 Hz
Channel 2	binary 0	1850 Hz
	binary 1	1650 Hz

Modulation techniques

This discussion is only related to techniques currently used in MODEMs on the PSTN.

Frequency shift keying (FSK)

The digital data is recoded as frequencies. The binary signal, such as V24 voltage levels, can only have two values, so only two frequencies are needed. This technique is used on slower MODEMs. In FSK the two values of voltage are converted into one of two different frequencies; this is done by a modulator.

The electrical circuit *modulates* the input voltage to produce the output. The receiver performs the opposite process, it takes in the frequency signal and *demodulates* it to produce the original voltage signal. Using this technique on the telephone lines is fairly easy; the frequencies can be in the range 3003300 Hz so they are easily passed through the PSTN just as if they were speech signals.

The major problem lies in the choice of frequencies, for which there are a number of constraints.

— The chosen frequencies have to be fairly far apart on the frequency range. That is, the cycle time for one should be measurably different from the other.

— In order to detect the actual frequency, half a wave, or cycle, must be transmitted. This means the input digital wave cannot change faster than twice the lowest frequency output from the modulator. Thus the lowest frequency used must be greater than the baud rate of the data signal.

— Certain frequency ranges on the telephone circuit are reserved for use by the switching equipment.

— The higher frequencies on a telephone circuit are attenuated.

Phase modulation

A newer technique that is used to provide a higher information rate whilst using the same frequencies involves coding the data into the phase of a wave. Remember that phase is measured between two waves; it can also be measured between the same signal wave at different points in time. If a wave has phase p_1 at time t_1, we can measure the phase at time t_2 relative to the phase at time t_1. It is very difficult to measure small changes in phase, so MODEMs mainly use large changes. If channel 1 is used by one MODEM to transmit on a connection it must be used by the other MODEM for receiving, and vice versa.

The timesharing MODEM can be used at either end of a connection, terminal or computer. A mechanism is needed to decide which channel should be used for transmitting and which channel for receiving at each end. By international agreement the following mechanism is used. When a MODEM is switched on, but before being connected for a data transfer, it is set to transmit on channel 1 and receive on channel 2. One of the MODEMs in a connection pair must change if data transfer is to proceed: by agreement this is the MODEM associated with the called computer or terminal. The normal situation is for the computer MODEM to be called by the user. Where a MODEM may be used to receive a call, such as at a computer site, the MODEM is arranged so that the incoming call switches the called MODEM over.

This type of MODEM arrangement is the most commonly used; it has been arranged so that a device known as an acoustic coupler can be used to replace the caller's MODEM. An acoustic coupler does not need installation directly into the telephone system. An acoustic coupler uses the same frequencies as the ordinary MODEM, but instead of placing them directly on to the telephone line it whistles into the mouthpiece of a telephone handset and takes the received signals from the earpiece. The acoustic coupler is a very cheap and convenient way of connecting a terminal to any telephone. Unfortunately, using the handset allows other noises from the room to interfere, so it is not as reliable as an installed MODEM.

Higher-speed asynchronous MODEM

Sometimes a faster rate of data transfer is required, say for printing messages, though the input may still be slow. The bandwidth available on the PSTN is not sufficient, given the noise, to allow a full duplex connection faster than 300 bps. However, research is continuing on modulation techniques to achieve faster data rates. A second type of MODEM is used to provide a higherspeed in one direction, but a much lower speed in the other direction. Up to 600 bps can be guaranteed on the PSTN in the UK, passing through the exchange in one direction, whilst the return channel has only 75 bps. The return channel is called a 'supervisory channel' and is not expected to carry much data.

Up to 1200 bps may be obtained using a dial-up connection if the noise is very low, but a 'private circuit' will provide a guaranteed 1200 bps. If a connection of 600/1200 bps is needed in both directions, then two MODEMs are needed at each end. If the PSTN is used via a dial-up line only a half duplex connection is possible, because the circuit can only manage 600/1200 bps in one direction at a time. If a private four-wire circuit is used then a full duplex connection is possible. Because the direction of the main data transfer is fixed, one type of

MODEM is used for sending on the fast channel (600/1200 bps) and receiving the supervisory channel (75 bps), whilst a different model performs the reverse operation at the other end. The 600/1200 MODEM uses frequency shift keying as the modulation technique, with the following: frequencies.

Up to 600 bps	binary 1	1300 Hz
	binary 0	1700 Hz
Up to 1200 bp	binary 1	1300 Hz
	binary 0	2100 Hz

The receiving MODEM can always tell if the sender is using 600 or 1200 bps as the idle frequency is different for the two data rates. Note that the frequency range 13002 100 Hz fills the middle of the available frequencies on the PSTN. This means that the supervisory channel is relegated to using the low frequencies, and therefore has a low data rate. The frequencies for the supervisory channel are

binary 1	390 Hz
binary 0	450 Hz

The dial-up MODEM using 1200/75 bps is becoming popular for use with teletex services.

Fast synchronous MODEM

A popular speed for synchronous transfer is 2400 bps. This is provided by a group of MODEMs that use differential phase encoding to obtain the higher data rate within the frequency range of the PSTN. The connection pattern is the same as for the 600/1200 bps MODEM; a simplex connection is available on the two-wire circuit via the exchange with a sending and receiving MODEM.

If a sending and receiving MODEM are provided at each end, a half duplex connection can be made by sharing the two-wire circuit. A full duplex connection can be obtained by using a private four-wire circuit. A 2400 bps MODEM is available for use over the PSTN using a dial-up line, but may be limited to 1200 bps by noise. The 2400 bps main data connection can be augmented by a 75 bps supervisory channel in the reverse direction, as in the 600/1200 MODEM. The differential phase encoding uses four possible phase changes on a 1200 Hz signal to obtain the 2400 bps data rate. MODEM speeds of 4800 bps and 9600 bps are also available, but only using private circuits.

Very high-speed MODEMs

For use in inter-computer communications, an arrangement is available for data rates between 40.8K bps and 50K bps over 48 kHz wide band circuits. Some of the larger exchanges in the PSTN are connected by very wide band circuits. These can be utilised for data transfer, although a private high-speed circuit may have bypassed several exchanges on the way to the large exchange. For the high-speed circuit four MODEMS are used, one pair to reach the large exchange, and another pair at the other end. Between the end pairs of MODEMs the data is passed in the base band frequency of the data signals on a special private circuit.

The main uses of MODEMs are listed below.

1. To connect a teletype or slow VDU (110/300 bps) to any computer in full duplex, by dialling through the PSTN.

2. To connect a faster terminal (600/1200 bps); but to get a full duplex connection a permanent private circuit is needed, so only one computer can be used.
3. To provide a synchronous connection using higher data rates (1200/2400, 4800, 9600 bps); but again a private circuit is needed for full duplex and full speed operation.
4. A very high data rate can be achieved, but at a higher cost, using base band signalling for part of the distance on a special circuit.

In terms of cost the acoustic coupler represents the cheapest modulation equipment. The cost then rises through the four types of MODEM described above. The higher the data rate, the higher the cost; however, the relationship is not linear. A 1200 bps service does not cost four times as much as a 300 bps service: it is more likely to cost only about twice as much to install, especially if a private wire is needed, but the rental may only be half as much again. Thus the problem of obtaining the optimum cost/service is not easy.

Digital Data Network

So far in this chapter we have been concerned with using an analogue PSTN that was designed to carry speech signals. The PTTs are currently investing very large sums of money in converting the existing analogue telephone equipment to use digital technology.

This digital telephone service is known as ISDN; there is an international standard for this service which includes the interface for connecting private equipment. In the UK, British Telecom are installing equipment to provide the ISDN service in a number of new exchanges and gradually replacing old exchanges and equipment.

The new digital systems convert the analogue speech signal into digital signals using a technique called 'pulse code modulation'. The encoded speech signals are carried through the network as digital signals and converted back to their analogue form for the receiver. Using digital signals for transferring analogue information has a number of advantages.

a. The effects of noise are considerably reduced.

b. Digital multiplexing techniques can be used to make more efficient use of the trunk network.

c. The subscriber circuits can be switched by digital processors using information embedded in the encoded signal.

d. The very cheap VLSI technology developed for computers can be used, thus allowing considerable intelligence to be built into the telephone network.

A further advantage for users of computer communications is that the PSTN can be used directly, and therefore more efficiently. The digital information from the computer is passed directly into the digital network where it is transferred in its original form.

The basic ISDN connection consists of two 64K bps channels, primarily for speech, and an 8K bps channel for control. It is expected that the control channel will be available for data use; this will have a major impact on home computing and personal information services. If required, either or both of the 64K bps channels can be used for data as well.

Standards

The PTTs from all over the world work through a body called the CCITT. The CCITT is a part of the United Nations. It is concerned with enabling the individual PTTs from all over the world to cooperate and provide an international service. The CCITT is one of the most authoritative standards organisations in communications, so any standard adopted by the CCITT is very important.

All of the MODEMs discussed in this chapter conform to international standards for their operation, so it is possible for a terminal user in the UK to use a timesharing computer in Germany by dialling the computer. The German computer uses a German MODEM, while the UK user has a UK MODEM, but because they conform to the same standards they will be able to operate together. The CCITT have had a tremendous impact on computer communications by standardising various interfaces between computing equipment. The most important interface is that between the MODEM and the user's equipment. For instance, for asynchronous terminals the interface standard is called V24. The V24 standard defines all of the control and data signals used to enable the MODEM and the user's equipment to operate together and pass data, including the signal levels.

The result of the standards and their widespread adoption by equipment manufacturers means that any terminal having a V24 interface can be plugged into any MODEM, anywhere. Furthermore computer manu-facturers now use the V24 standard for connecting local terminals as well. This compatibility between equipment is very important in allowing various different types of equipment, from different manufacturers, to be interchangeable. Because the manufacturers in the United

States dominate the computer industry the standards adopted by the United States often become the international standards of the CCITT. One of the US standards called RS232C is in fact the same as the V24 recommendation and preceded it. RS232C was the name given to the standard in the US before it became an international recommendation. Many US manufacturers still refer to it as RS232C rather than V24. The CCITT have defined a standard interface for connecting communications equipment to a digital switched network: this standard is known as X.21. A second interface standard, known as X.21(bis), allows the same mechanisms but over the analogue PSTN, because there are still so few digital services available. The packet switched network access interface, X.25, is defined to used X.21 as its lowest level. However, X.21 (bis), or even V24, may be used where a digital network is not yet available.

Computer network technology

Terminal networks are all built around a central computer; similarly remote job entry stations are usually connected to a single computer. In the remaining chapters some of the problems and techniques of a network of inter-communicating devices are discussed. The devices at present connected to networks are usually general-purpose computers, with their own terminal networks. One reason for networking multiaccess computers, rather than terminals or smaller devices, is that these computer systems already existed when networking was proposed. A second reason is that the protocols used in computer networks are very complex so that only a large computer system would have sufficient spare computing power to implement them. However, terminals can be directly attached to a network, by using a dedicated computer. In the near future computer networks will become as widespread as the telephone network, and large scale integration will enable cheap processors to handle the protocols. The result will be the networking of every sort of computing device. The current trends indicate that powerful, single user, workstations will replace terminals for network use. The workstations will be directly connected to a local area network and use the resources of larger computers via the network. This chapter is primarily concerned with the technology used to connect the computers and devices that make up a computer network. For the purposes of description the range of technology has been divided into three areas

1. wide area networks
2. Radio and satellite broadcast networks
3. Local networks

The network technology includes the techniques used to interconnect the computing devices and physically transfer information from one computing device to another.

Wide area networks

The term 'wide area network' is applied to a network that covers a large physical area, say a whole country or large area under one administration. Such an area may be worldwide where a multinational organisation owns the network. The basic communication media used are dedicated circuits, usually of about 50 kHz bandwidth. Where digital circuits are available the bandwidth would be 64K bps. The recent introduction of fibre optics in longdistance trunks has make link bandwidth of 2-3M bps available. Wide area networks will be using these links over the next few years. Examples of such networks are PSS, ARPANET, Tymnet, Telenet, etc.; details of some of these networks are given at the end of this section. For reasons explained in chapter 3, the physical circuits are usually provided by a PTT, although in the case of PSS the whole network is also run by the PTT.

Although 50 kHz bandwidth seems to be a lot compared with the 3 kHz nominal bandwidth of the voice telephone line, it is not very much when highspeed or large-volume transfers of information are required. Even at these high speeds the channel capacity is a resource that needs to be used efficiently.

It is now necessary to see how information can be transferred from one computer to any other on the network. The problem falls into two parts. The first is that of transferring information via a medium, such as a wire. The second part is concerned with addressing and routing. If there were only two computers on a network, then they could be connected by two channels, one for each direction, and whatever one computer transmitted the other would be bound to receive.

When more computers are added, the bidirectional connection solution can be extended by having each computer connected to every other computer by a full duplex connection. To send a message to a particular computer the appropriate connection is selected; thus the routing of a message is carried out by the sender. Using a dedicated connection between every computer on the network is very expensive. If there are n computers on the network then $n(n-1)/2$ lines are needed, and have to be paid for! As a single computer would not normally be communicating with every other computer on the network at the same time, most of the lines would be unused in a fully connected network. Therefore to increase the utilisation of the connection circuits, their number is reduced, and switching is introduced within the network. There are three forms of switching that can be used in communications: circuit switching, message switching, and packet switching.

Circuit switching

Circuit switching is used on the PSTN to connect telephone subscribers. To use it for a computer network each computer would have a private circuit to a local exchange, and the exchanges would be connected to form a network. Whenever two computers wish to exchange information, a physical path is established between them via the exchanges. The path is then disconnected when the connection is closed. The circuit has been ,switched' by the exchanges. This method of connection is not used on established computer networks. The major disadvantages of circuit switching are

1. The cost of the equipment is very high, whereas the resulting circuit is not necessarily of high enough quality for computer communications.
2. The resulting circuit can only be used by the two computers on the call, thus the equipment is dedicated to the circuit. In particular the connection from the computer to the exchange is dedicated. To enable a single computer to communicate with more than one other computer at the same time, extra equipment is needed for each simultaneous call. If there are no connections all the equipment is idle but being paid for.

3. The time taken to set up the physical path can be very long in computer terms.

As high-speed connection using good-quality circuits is important for efficient computer networks, circuit switching is discounted in favour of the other methods. Circuit switching is used for some networks connecting computers-for instance, the Nordic Data Network.

Circuit switching has two advantages

1. Charges are made only for the time that a call is connected. If infrequent and short connections are all that is required, then circuit switching may be advantageous to the customer. It is expected that many slower devices, such as terminals, will be connected to national computer networks via the PSTN to gain this advantage.

2. Where a single device is used for long periods, such as a facsimile machine, circuit switching is economically advantageous. This is particularly true where digital facilities, such as X.21, are available.

When the ISDN service is widely available, then it will be an attractive mechanism for some computer networks. Each host will be able to set up calls, use the 64K bps bandwidth, and quickly close the call, as required. The circuits will still carry packets for the end-to-end data transfer; but circuit switching will be the main link-switching mechanism.

Message switching

To overcome problems in setting up and taking down physical circuits via exchanges, computer networks use permanent circuits and switch the data, A partially connected network is used in which each computer has a permanent circuit to a number of its neighbours, but not to all computers on the network. An example will illustrate the basic operation of *information switching* where the unit of information is a message.

If the computer at A wishes to send a message to B, the message must pass through either D or C. The points on the network are called *nodes. A will* address the message to B by placing the address of B in the message header. The message and address are then sent on the circuit to D. At D the node inspects the address; if the address is 'D' the message is given to the computer; if the address is not D the message is forwarded on a circuit that the node believes will enable the message to be delivered, In this case D will forward the message to B. Thus the node at D has switched the message on to the appropriate output circuit. In this example two major characteristics of a computer network can be seen.

— *Addressing:* The message is addressed to a remote destination and sent on the next stage of its route.

— *Store and Forward*: Each message is received into the node storage so that it can be processed as a whole unit. Usually an error check is carried out and the whole message has to be received before this can be completed. The message is then inspected for routing information so that the node can decide which output circuit to use to forward the message.

The nodes have been introduced in the network to carry out the functions of routing and store and forward, so the host computer is separated from the network operation as much as possible. The 'hosts' are the user computers which wish to use the network. Often a number of hosts will be attached to a single node.

The node computers are usually minicomputers chosen for their ability to respond in real time to the communications devices. Each node receives incoming messages and stores them. When a complete message has been received the destination address is inspected so that the message can be placed on the output queue of a circuit to forward the message.

If the message is for a host attached to the node, the output circuit will be the one connected to the host. If the message is for a distant host the node must forward the message to another node on the route to the distant host. While the message is in the node store, waiting to be processed or waiting for output, it is, of course, being delayed. The link into any one node may be used to carry messages from several different computers, as may the connection between the node and host. The physical equipment involved is used more efficiently than in circuit switching as a result of this multiplexing. Message multiplexing is the most important advantage of message and packet switching computer networks.

To distinguish between message and packet switching it is necessary to understand what a message is. This has already been introduced in earlier chapters, but a more detailed discussion is given here.

The easiest way of defining a message is to say that it is a unit of information which is exchanged by users of a network. This means the characteristics of a message are only dependent on the user or the application. A message could be a few bits or a file, or even a whole database. In a message-switching network the whole message is passed from one node to another as a complete entity. Compared with circuit switching, a message-switching network has the following characteristics.

1. Any computer can communicate with any other computer without having a direct physical connection.
2. Any computer can communicate with several others using the same equipment by multiplexing messages.
3. There is no delay arising from circuit set up, but messages are delayed when they pass through a node *enroute.*

The messages can be transferred between nodes, and nodes and hosts, using an *ARQ* protocol. Characteristic 3 implies that there is no delay arising from the use of a network other than the store and forward operation of the nodes. This is true in some networks using pure datagram techniques.

However, in most networks the internode protocol used within the network introduces some delays. Any network using a virtual circuit protocol, at any level, will introduce a delay when the message or packet is given to the network. In many networks the local node negotiates for resources within the network before actually forwarding a message. This is true of an X.25 network when the call is first set up, and is true of every message on the ARPA network. A user of a message-switching network will pass the network a message, together with a destination address, and the user will receive messages as single units.

The advantages of message switching, over circuit switching are

— The sender may dispatch the message when convenient, even if the receiver is not ready, as the network will store the message for delivery, However, if network resources run out, an undelivered message may be deleted and thus lost; this depends on the network protocols.

— Computers can exchange information at different speeds, as the network will buffer the message.

— Broadcasting of a message may be possible.

— Equipment is used more efficiently.

— Messages may be handled by priority.

Each message is treated as a single unit. However, there are also some disadvantages.

— A very long message will hold up other, perhaps more urgent, messages as it monopolises a circuit for the duration of its transmission.

— As a message may be very large, the node computer may not have enough memory to store it before forwarding it; in this case the message is lost. Further, this message will never be delivered as the network does not have the required resources.

— A very large message may monopolise the storage of a node, because it cannot be delivered, so that other messages cannot be received by this node.

Packet switching

The disadvantages of message switching relate to the possible occurrence of *large* messages, where the exact value of 'large' will depend on the network. If a network could be certain of only handling small messages, the disadvantages would disappear. The transfer of messages is a user requirement, so a network that meets user needs must be able to handle very large messages as well as small messages. The solution to these two conflicting requirements is to break the user's message into small *packets* for transfer through the network and have the packets reassembled into the message by the receiver. Note that the message header is included as the data in the first packet and that each packet has its own header. This refinement produces packet switching, which is the most widely used switching technique for computer networks. The physical organisation of a packet-switching network is the same as for message switching. The network is a partially connected mesh of nodes. For practical reasons most wide area networks use special node computers to perform the switching, with the user computers being attached to the nodes.

The term 'host' is now widely used to mean a user computer system attached to a network. The nodes are part of the network, so the hosts use a well-defined interface for accessing the node to enable data transfer across the network. By using a node separated from the host, all of the packet-switching functions, such as storage and routing, are removed from the host. However, the host still needs considerable software to handle the protocols used to access the node and to transfer data to other computers on the network.

The advantages that packet switching has over message switching are

- The small maximum packet size makes storage allocation and management easier in the switching nodes, sufficiently so for minicomputers to be used.
- The multiplexing of packets enables several messages to be interleaved on one circuit, reducing the delay seen by the user.

— The total transmission time through the network is reduced. Figure shows a message passing from A to B which would normally require 6k + d seconds to reach B, where 3k is the transmission time of the whole message on one link and d is the node delay. If the message is broken into three packets, each taking k seconds to transmit, the whole message arrives at B in 4k + d seconds. The difference increases with the number of links traversed and the size of the message.

Packet switching solves all the problems of wide area network organisation: it uses fixed highspeed lines and minicomputers for nodes; it is also more efficient and responsive than message switching. However, although packet switching is a better technique with which to implement a computer network, users still want to transfer messages. Packet switching introduces another layer of complexity and translation between the user and the physical network transporting the bits.

Fortunately, the cost of processing is falling so the extra cost is outweighed by the practical advantages. A second cost, not so easily overcome, is that each packet will have its own overheads as well as those used by each message; this will reduce the efficiency of the physical circuits. The conclusion drawn from consideration of these three switching techniques is that packet switching, especially used in a partially connected mesh of nodes with wideband circuits, is currently the best technique for wide area computer networks.

Packet switching is also used in other network technologies, rather than message switching, for the same reasons. Wide area networks have been in existence since the early 1970s. The best known example is the ARPA network in the United States. This network was established by a government research agency to link together computer centres that had contracts for government research so that research workers could share the available computing resources. The network itself also forms part of a research project to evaluate the feasibility of a large computer network, and to investigate techniques that could be used in such a network.

The ARPA network has been very successful in showing that the concept of resource sharing by use of a network is feasible. One of the most noticeable advantages that the network has introduced is a mail facility. This allows each user with access to a computer on the network to exchange mail with all the other network users. The mail facility is probably one of the main sources of traffic on the ARPA network and has certainly improved the amount of communication between researchers at different sites.

The basic techniques used within the ARPA network have been influenced by the defence aspects of the research, particularly the need for a fast response and resilience to the failure of any part. The network consists of a mesh of partially connected nodes called Interface Message Processors (IMPs). Each IMP can have up to eight hosts connected to it and may be connected to up to eight other IMPs. Each IMP accepts messages from the hosts of up to 8K bits in length.

The IMP breaks the message into IK bit packets which are then forwarded through the network of IMPs to the IMP attached to the destination host. This destination IMP reassembles the message before delivering it to the destination host. If a host wishes to send a message of more than 8K bits it must break the message up itself, into

8K packets, and the destination host must reassemble the message from the 8K packets. Thus the translation between messages and packets takes place at two levels. Within the network of IMPs, packets (1K) are sent individually along whichever route is best at the time, so that packets in a single message may use different routes and may arrive at the destination IMP out of sequence.

The destination IMP has to reassemble the message from the packets as they arrive. However, messages passed from the host to the IMP are delivered in the same sequence to the destination host. The technology developed for the ARPANET is now used in a number of commercial wide area networks all over the world.

The British Telecom network PSS (Packet Switching Stream) is an example of a network provided by a PTT as a public service. The design requirements for such a network are different from those of the ARPA network so they have resulted in a network with different characteristics. The network topology consists of a number of *exchanges* which are also partially connected. Each exchange is connected to a number of host computers in its area. The exchanges contain the node computers, the number of node computers in each exchange depending on the number of hosts attached to the exchange.

The hosts use an access protocol called X.25 to enable them to make virtual calls to other hosts. A host will give the local exchange the destination address of the host with which it wishes to communicate. The network will route the call to the destination exchange which will then complete the call to the destination host. The call is represented by information kept at all the exchanges on the route. The information is then used to forward the packets transferred on the call. Once the call has been established the hosts may exchange their own information. This is very similar to circuit switching on the PSTN although it is provided using packet-switching techniques. The PSS network techniques are different from those on the ARPA network, where each message is addressed and transferred separately. The hosts can use a single link to the PSS exchange to carry a number of virtual calls to other hosts, thus the link is used to multiplex the calls.

Broadcast networks

Broadcast networks use a channel to which all the users are connected, so all the users receive any transmission made on the channel. At present the two types of channel in use are local radio, covering up to a few hundred kilometres, and satellite channels which are used to span very large distances. Networks using radio and satellite channels have special problems because noise in the channel can cause errors. There is also the problem of allocating the channel for transmission. The first operational broadcast computer network was built at the University of Hawaii using local radio transmission; many of the techniques and much of the terminology derive from this first network. Every node receives all packets transmitted on the broadcast channel. When the received packet is complete, the node checks the packet for errors and then checks the destination address. If the address of the receiver matches the packet destination address, it is accepted; otherwise it is discarded. The problems particular to a broadcast network occur in the allocation of the channel to a node for transmitting a packet. Different solutions are used for radio and satellite links. Each node is only able to communicate with each other node via the common channel, so some scheme is needed to coordinate transmission. The schemes that have been proposed and used are discussed here in increasing complexity and are compared for channel efficiency. The simplest transmission technique is called *pure aloha;* when a node has a packet to transmit it does so immediately. Having transmitted the packet, the node waits for an acknowledgement. This is therefore a positive acknowledgement protocol. If an acknowledgement is not received within a time out period, the packet is assumed lost.

Transmission collisions, which occur when two nodes transmit at the same time and thus interfere with each other's transmission, are detected by the time out mechanism. When a collision is detected, each node waits a period of time of random length before retransmitting the packet to of traffic increases, the rate of collision will increase and more re-transmissions will be needed. As the older packets are re-transmitted, more stations will have newer packets to transmit, causing more collisions, etc.

Analysis has shown that a pure aloha scheme can only use a maximum of about 18% of the channel bandwidth. A node may transmit at any time, thus the maximum length of time the channel is wasted as a result of a collision is 2t, where t is the transmission time for one packet. The 2t period is the worst case, where one node begins transmitting just before the previous transmission is complete. An improvement on pure aloha is *slotted aloha* in which the transmission channel time is divided into time slots of *t*.

Each node is then only allowed to begin transmitting a packet at the start of a time slot. The nodes are kept in synchronisation by a time signal on the channel. Now if a collision occurs only one slot *is* wasted, so the maximum efficiency rises to about 34% of the channel capacity. When a collision is detected, a transmitter must wait for a random number of time slots before retransmitting. When the traffic is light the wait can be quite short, but as the traffic load increases the waiting period should be increased. From the aloha schemes it can be seen that it is collisions that cause problems, so a collision avoidance mechanism should improve efficiency. In packet radio networks a scheme known as Carrier Sense Multiple Access (CSMA) is used. When a node is transmitting all other nodes can receive the transmission, so they can avoid a collision by not transmitting themselves until the channel is free. A transmission is detected by the presence of the carrier signal in the medium. When a node has a packet to transmit it looks for the carrier; if there is no carrier the packet is transmitted. If the carrier is detected the node waits for a random length delay and tries again.

Even in a radio broadcast the signal from a transmitter takes a finite amount of time to reach all the receivers in the network. When two nodes find the channel free, they may both begin transmission because neither has heard the other one. This case is most likely to happen when two stations are waiting for the channel to become free. The length of time it takes to propagate the signal to all receivers is the time band in which collisions may occur, but it is less than the total packet transmission time. As with the aloha technique, the CSMA technique can be improved by dividing the channel time into slots and only allowing the transmission of packets to begin at the start of a time slot. The slot length is set to the propagation delay, not the packet transmission time. The CSMA technique has been further refined by modifying the action of the node when the channel is busy. When the node samples the channel again and finds it free, it transmits its packet with a probability p, or waits for a further delay of random length, with a probability (1-p). This is called persistent CSMA or p-persistent transmission. If p is high then the delay before transmission occurs is lower, but the possibility of collision increases if two stations are waiting for another station to finish.

In persistent CSMA a trade off is made between channel efficiency and delay with the value of p. Channel efficiencies of about 80% may be achieved using these techniques. Packet radio networks have a small delay between the start of a transmission and the detection of the transmission by all stations on the network. On a satellite broadcast network there is a very long delay between transmission and receiving, of the order of a quarter of a second.

A satellite network operates by each transmitter sending its signal to the satellite. The satellite then broadcasts the signal to all of the Earth stations, which may be spread over a very large area. One satellite system currently used for packet switching connects nodes in England, Norway and North America using a satellite in stationary orbit over the North Atlantic.

A different channel allocation technique is used on satellite broadcast networks because of the long propagation delay. This satellite channel allocation technique involves making reservations for the future use of slots in the channel. The channel is divided into frames consisting of a number of reservation slots and a number of packet slots. Each reservation slot represents a packet slot in the second part of the frame.

All ground stations are synchronised to the frame timing by the satellite transmission. During the first part of the frame the ground stations reserve slots for the packets they have ready by transmitting a marker during the reservation slot time. When the reservation slot is heard on the satellite down channel, the ground station inspects the slot to see if it contains its own marker. If so it can transmit a packet in the corresponding packet slot in the second part of the frame. This scheme uses some of the channel capacity to avoid the collisions which could reduce the network to a pure aloha scheme.

Obviously more than one ground station may attempt to reserve a particular packet slot by transmitting during the reservation slot time. There are a number of algorithms to overcome this, including allocating some slots to busy stations. Thus if a station successfully obtained a packet slot in the last frame, the same slot is allocated to that station in the next frame without competition. If an allocated slot is not used then the slot is open for competition in the following frame. Usually there are some slots that all stations can compete for in every frame. Another mechanism involves using a central allocation station to which each station sends its requirements and the central station allocates the slots. This has two disadvantages: firstly, the central station becomes a weakness in the network reliability, and secondly, the delay between requesting an allocation and receiving the allocation may be of the order of 1 or 2 seconds before the packet can be transmitted.

Local area networks

A local network is a communication system connecting computers in a small geographical area, say less than a few kilometres between the furthest points. The network is wholly owned and run by one administration. There are currently two basic types of technology used on such a network: these are cable, or bus, technology and ring technology.

Whereas wide area networks and satellite networks use nodes to separate the internal network switching from the user hosts, local networks are meant to be as cheap as possible and so the separate node computer is omitted. In both local network t2logies all the computers are directly attached to the transmission medium by a special interface, and all the interfaces receive all the packets. The difference between a ring and a bus system is the way in which the channel is allocated.

Local networks are designed for use in local computing by allowing the interconnection of very small computers, such as microprocessors, personal workstations and peripheral devices. If the local network is to be useful, the cost of the computer interfaces into the network channel has to be low compared with the cost of the computer or peripheral, and microprocessors are very cheap in computer terms.

A widely forecast use of local networks is connecting word processors within a set of offices for the exchange of information and electronic mail. The cost constraints, the limited processing power of the small computers and the protocols used on a local network are different from those used in wide area networks. A local network usually has a very high bandwidth channel of between I and 10 MHz and a very low error rate say one bit in several million might be corrupted. These characteristics permit the use of simple protocols.

Cable or bus networks

These networks usually use a length of coaxial cable, or an existing cable such as that used for closed circuit television (CCTV). The medium is used in a broadcast fashion, exactly as described in the previous section on broadcast networks. The channel allocation techniques vary slightly on the theme of the CSMA techniques, or on a centralised slot allocation. The most popular broadcast local network is the Ethernet system developed by Xerox. The Ethernet principles can be used on any broadcast medium: radio, telephone lines, coaxial cable and optical fibres have all been used successfully.

The Ethernet uses a base band signal, rather than a modulated signal, to simplify the broadcast transmitter and receiver, with a modified CSMA channel access technique. To obtain the maximum efficiency from the broadcast medium an Ethernet transmitter can listen to its own broadcast to detect a collision and abort the transmission. This extra complexity is known as CSMACD (CD = collision detection) or listen-while-talk. As with the other CSMA techniques a station does not begin transmitting until the broadcast medium is free. Two stations waiting for another station to finish a transmission will begin transmitting together, and thus interfere with each other.

The collision is detected by the stations and they both abort the transmission immediately. To enforce the protocol a station that aborts a transfer then jams the ether. After a collision each station waits for a random time before trying again. The CSMA-CD technique enables the Ethernet system to obtain up to 95% of the broadcast channel bandwidth. The improvement in performance over ordinary CSMA is due to the stopping of transmission as soon as a collision is detected. Note that no slots are used so a network-wide timing signal is not required. The transceiver handles all of the CSMACD access, including the retries and delay calculation which is varied with the traffic load. Thus only complete, and checked, packets are passed up to the station interface and only one request is made for a packet to be sent. The checksum generation and checking are carried out within the hardware: bad packets are discarded. A time out mechanism is used to retransmit packets that may have been lost as a result of errors.

Ring networks

The ring technique originated in the USA. The idea was then developed in parallel at Cambridge University in the UK and at two research centres in the USA. The version developed at Cambridge is known as the Cambridge ring in the UK. The computer interface is divided into two parts: the repeater and the interface proper. A ring uses a twisted pair of wires as the transmission medium.

However, to improve reliability, the repeater is powered from the ring and electrically isolated from the computer interface, so four wires are used to connect the repeaters. The four wires are used as two pairs for signalling and carry sufficient power for the repeaters. In this way the computer can be switched off and removed from the ring without switching off the repeater. With the ring the medium is terminated at each station, whereas in the cable network it is not. Each station is represented by a repeater, several of which are then connected together into a ring.

The repeater is a simple device containing a shift register and some logic to detect certain conditions in the information being passed around the ring. The repeater normally passes any information received on to the next repeater, so transmission only occurs in one direction. When a station transmits data, the repeater transmits the information from the station instead of the information received from the previous repeater.

Slotted ring

There are slight differences in the channel allocation mechanism used in the Cambridge ring and in those rings developed in the USA. In the Cambridge ring a fixed-size mini-packet is used which constantly circulates in the ring, and a special station called a monitor is used to ~generate and maintain the mini-packet and provide the power for the repeaters. In the American versions a variable-size packet is used which may be lost and regenerated as required by each repeater. The current format of the Cambridge mini-packet. Note that only 16 bits of information are carried in a ring mini-packet whereas the broadcast network packet may contain several hundred bytes.

The assembly of information into a block has to be done by the computer. The monitor station also provides a buffer if the ring is not physically long enough to hold a complete mini-packet. The monitor performs a check on the mini-packet each time it passes to ensure that it is intact, and to replace it if not. The monitor is an obvious weakness in the Cambridge ring design so far as reliability is concerned; however, experience so far has shown that monitor failures are rare. The advantage of the monitor is that the repeaters can be very simple as well as cheap, which is the purpose of a local network. To use the ring to send a packet of information, the station will wait until an empty mini-packet is detected by the repeater.

When the full/empty bit in the mini-packet passes the repeater it is set to one. If the packet was already full no change has been made to the bit; if the packet was empty (full/empty bit = 0) the mini-packet is now reserved by this station, The repeater will use this mini-packet if the full/empty bit was received as 0. The addresses of the source and destination stations are placed in the address fields followed by the next 16 bits of the information that the station wishes to send; these are placed in the data field from the station buffer. The reserved mini-packet then travels round to all the other stations on the ring.

Each station has a source select register in which an address is placed. If the source address in a mini-packet matches the contents of the source select register, and the destination address matches the station address, the data field is copied into the station receive buffer and the accept status is set at the end of the packet. If the packet is refused, or the destination station is busy, the destination repeater will set the appropriate value in the status bits at the end of the mini-packet.

No other change is made by the receiving repeater, and all other repeaters will pass on the mini-packet unchanged. Special values which can be used in the source select register are: all ones, which means accept any source station address, and all zeros, which means do not accept the data from any mini-packets. When the mini-packet returns to the sending station the full/empty bit is reset to 0 and the status bits are checked to see if the information was accepted. As an error check, the station also reads back the 16 data bits and checks them against the data in its buffer. Having reset the full/empty bit, the station must now wait for another empty mini-packet before it can send the next 16 bits of information. In this way the now empty packet becomes available to successive stations around the ring and the packet slot is allocated in a round robin fashion.

The variable nature of packet traffic in a local network makes it difficult to design a system that will provide a very fast response, especially when there is little traffic, and yet not become overloaded or unfair when the traffic becomes heavy.

The broadcast techniques provide a low delay, especially in low-volume traffic, as the transmitter can usually send a packet as soon as one is available. However, as the volume of traffic increases, the broadcast system suffers from collisions and longer delays which can eventually lead to an unstable situation. In the slotted ring the channel is allocated by means of a round robin mechanism so collisions never occur, and during a burst of traffic each station is able to continue transmitting with only a larger delay.

During periods of low traffic volume the ring does introduce a delay while a station waits for the empty packet to come round. Proponents of both systems argue that because of the very high bandwidth available on the channel, and the low processing power of the computers attached to the local network, the volume of traffic is nearly always low in a broadcast network and the delay is negligible in a ring.

Token Ring

The token ring attempts to provide the advantages of broadcast access in low-volume traffic periods, with the inherent sharing of the slotted ring during high-volume traffic periods. The physical topology of the ring is the same, but instead of a circulating mini-packet there is a circulating token. Any host requiring access to the ring waits for the token to arrive; it then changes the token to indicate that a packet is following. The modified token is then followed immediately by the data packet, which can be of any size up to some system maximum. All hosts detect the modified token and examine the packet to see if it is addressed to them; if it is the packet is copied off the ring. The receiving host still sends the packet on though, so the data packet goes all the way round the ring to the sender.

The sender takes the packet off the ring. Normally the sender receives the front of the data packet before it has finished transmitting the rest of the packet, owing to the short length of the ring. When the receiver detects the end of the data packet it marks its status by changing the last few bits, as in the Cambridge ring mini-packet; thus the sender knows if the packet was accepted or not. Immediately the sender has finished the packet it puts a token on the ring so another host may have a go. The token ring is a simple idea, but it is more complex than the Cambridge ring and the interfaces are more expensive.

The initialise sequence which is required to start the ring is quite complex as the token has to be put on the ring to start data transfer; of course there can only be one token. The mechanisms for detecting duplicate tokens and lost tokens, without the use of a monitor station, add to the cost of the computer interfaces. IBM carried out extensive tests and simulations of all the local area network technologies, and decided that the token ring was the best available. The company now intends to use the token ring as the basis of its local area network products. The protocols used in a computer network are the mechanisms by which the hosts exchange information over physical distances.

In the OSI model, the network layer is the primary layer for host-to-host communication. The network layer makes use of services from the link and physical layers; it also provides an end-to-end service to the transport layer. The network layer can utilise a number of physical networks to provide its services. The two services provided by the network layer are the connectionless services, and the connection-orientated service. X.25 protocol is important as it is being used on all public packet-switched networks operated by the PTTs. The X.25 protocol defines the necessary operation of layers one, two and three.

The X.25 protocol

Within any layer, a connection orientated protocol has two common tasks: error control and flow control. Error control is concerned with detecting, and correcting, errors that may have occurred in the information being transferred. Flow control is concerned with managing the resources of bandwidth and storage so that no single user can monopolise these resources, and the two endpoints are kept in step with each other. This is usually achieved by keeping the sending and receiving rates of information transfer approximately in step.

The X.25 protocol covers the three lower layers of the protocol hierarchy. X.25 is defined as an access protocol, which means that it is used between a host and a node (in most X.25 networks the nodes are called 'exchanges') for the host to access the network so that communication between remote hosts is possible. The X.25 protocol has been adopted by the CCITT as a standard, which means that nearly all future networks will use it. The latest version of X.25 will be adopted by ISO as an international standard.

As well as describing the particulars of X.25, the principles of error and flow control will be shown and the mechanisms used to implement them in each layer explained. The description of level 2 is very detailed, as this is the first consequential level to be met in the bottom-up approach. The discussion of level 2 examines a number of problems which occur at many other protocol layers.

For instance, the mechanisms used at level 3 for flow control and protocol synchronisation are very similar to those of level 2, so less detail is given in the level 3 explanation and references are made to the level 2 mechanisms. In the X.25 parlance a host is called a DTE (Data Terminating Equipment) and a node is called a DCE (Data Communications Equipment). X.25 provides a standard mechanism for a DTE to access and use a DCE to transport data across a network to a remote DTE via its remote DCE. The protocol used between the DCEs within the network does not have to be X.25, but would probably be very close to it. X.25 is a virtual call (connection-orientated) protocol.

This level provides the physical communication by specifying the electrical signals, voltages, plug shape and pin assignment that the DTE needs to connect physically to the DCE. This would be the normal arrangement, as the supplier of the network (usually the PTT) will provide the MODEM link to the node (DCE) from the user's premises. The actual specification of level I is contained in the CCITT X.21 recommendation.

For practical purposes the user will order a computer interface to this standard which plugs straight into the computer at one end and into the MODEM at the other. The user will normally also be able to buy the software necessary to handle the interface.

As the level 1 hardware is bought as a ready-made unit, no further discussion of it is necessary. The important information needed about level 1 is the type of interface it presents to level 2, and the functions it must perform. The level 1 will provide transport for a bit stream from the DTE to a (remote) DCE.

The level 2 will present the level 1 with the bits which are then delivered to a level 2 at the DCE. The hardware of level 1 will also indicate if the physical circuit is working correctly, that is whether the MODEMs are switched on and able to exchange synchronised data. So the interface has two parts

1. the sending and receiving of a serial bit stream
2. the control signals indicating the status of the physical circuit.

The purpose of level 2 is to control the physical link between the two ends of the level 1 circuit to provide a reliable transfer of information for level 3 between the DTE and DCE. X.25 level 2 uses a link control protocol based on the ISO HDLC (Higher Data Link Control) protocol. The advantages of using an existing protocol are greater than those to be gained from designing a new one. For instance, a new protocol would have to be adopted by a large number of people wishing to communicate; adoption of the protocol would then require a lot of effort. Other link protocols have been designed: IBM use one called SDLC (Synchronous Data Link Control) on their SNA network, which is not dissimilar to HDLC; DEC have their own as well.

Information is passed from level 2 to level 1 in blocks called 'frames'. The use of frames enables easier management of storage and error control. Each frame consists of some protocol information added by level 2, and possibly an information packet from level 3. 1 will use the convention of calling level 2 blocks frames and level 3 blocks *packets. The* functions performed by level 2 are

1. To establish the link connection to a level 2 at a remote site.
2. To transfer packets for level 3 securely, and in sequence.
3. To disconnect the link without loss of level 3 information.

To carry out these functions, the X. 25 level 2 uses three types of frame format. The uses of each format are shown in the next section, but first the fields in the frames are detailed

Flag field

This is a unique 8 bit pattern (01111110) which marks the beginning and end of each frame. The use of the flag as a delimiter presents a problem: to ensure that the end of the frame is correctly interpreted by the receiver, the flag pattern must not appear anywhere within the data in the frame. This means that the frame must be transparent to the hardware looking for a flag to mark the beginning or ending of a frame. The problem of transparency occurs in all link level protocols as they all use special bit patterns for synchronisation and for marking various parts of the frame. In X. 25 level 2 the flag is used as the level 1 synchronisation character (see chapter 2 on synchronous character frames).

To ensure that the flag pattern does not occur within the frame, X.25 uses a technique called 'bit stuffing'. The bit stuffing technique involves the sender in inspecting the frame contents prior to transfer to level 1. Whenever a sequence of five Is occurs a 0 is inserted. Notice that the 0 is inserted regardless of the value of the sixth bit. Bit stuffing in this way is easily implemented by hardware and only increases the length of the frame by 1 bit for every sequence of five Is.

As the receiving hardware scans the incoming frame, a 0 following a sequence of five Is is removed. If the sequence of five Is is followed by a further 1, then the flag may have been found. The seventh bit is then inspected: if it is a 0 the flag has been found (01111110), whereas if the seventh bit is another 1 (01111111) then the frame is in error. Thus a sequence of seven Is is used to abort the frame.

There are other ways of providing transparency, such as using escape characters, or bit counts, but none is quite so efficient and flexible as bit stuffing.

Address field

This is really redundant in a point-to-point link. The intention in the HDLC protocol was to use this as an address for multipoint lines, but the present X. 25 recommendation does not include multipoint lines. However, X.25 uses the field as an additional check in the protocol, as well as having the field ready should multipoint lines be considered in the future. The addresses used in this field allow commands and responses to be separated. The level 2 link can be thought of as two separate channels.

Channel A for transferring data from the network (DCE) to the host (DTE) and

Channel B for transferring data from the host (DTE) to the network (DCE).

Any frames relating to information flow from the DCE to the DTE carry the address A (11000000) including any frames from the DTE to the DCE relating to information transfer from the network to the host; similarly for channel B (10000000). To help separate the channels, frames are divided into two classes: *commands* and *responses*, Commands always flow in the direction of information on a channel; responses flow in the opposite direction. Responses are obviously the receiver's replies to various commands.

Command field

This 8 bit pattern determines the type of the frame, as well as being used for sequence numbering and acknowledgement. The command field has a different meaning for the three types of frame (information, supervisory, unnumbered). A 0 in bit 1 indicates that this is an information frame. An information frame is the only type that carries a level 3 packet in the information field.

Bits 2, 3 and 4 contain the sequence number of this frame, bits 6, 7 and 8 contain the acknowledgement number. The sequence number and acknowledgement number are used in the ARQ techniques explained in chapter 6 for error correction and flow control.

Level 2 uses a stop-go flow control. Bit 5 is the poll/final (P/F) bit. This is set in a command frame as a poll bit and the receiver will set the final bit in any response frame that is a reply to a command frame with the poll bit set. The use of the poll/final bit enables the sender of a command to recognise the corresponding response frame. Bits 1 and 2 set to 10 indicate a supervisory frame. Bits 3 and 4 indicate which type of supervisory frame, Supervisory frames are not given sequence numbers as they do not contain any level 3 information, but they may be used to acknowledge information frames and so bits 6, 7 and 8 contain an acknowledgement number. Bit 5 is the poll/final bit which is the same as before.

The command field format for the *unnumbered frame,* so called because it contains neither sequence number nor acknowledgement number. Bits 1 and 2 set to 11 indicate an unnumbered frame and bit 5 is the poll/final bit. The remainder of the bits are used to indicate the type of unnumbered frame

Information field

This field only occurs in information frames; it is the position in the frame where the whole level 3 packet is placed. The other level 2 fields provide an envelope for the level 3 packet during the level 2 transfer.

Frame check sequence

The FCS field is found by counting 16 bits back from the terminating flag. This is a 16 bit field to contain the CRC remainder used in error checking. The remainder is calculated using the CCITT recommended generating polynomial of $X^{16} + X^{12} + X^5 + 1$. It is interesting to note that all the fields of the X.25 level 2 header and the CRC are multiples of 8 bits. This makes transmission easier, because the 8 bit byte is the lowest common multiple of most modern computer word sizes, as well as being the character frame size for synchronous transfer. However the information field and the CRC may be increased by bit stuffing for level 1 transmission. This section describes the semantics of level 2, with the various commands and responses being explained in context. The level 2 at the DTE (host) end of the connection performs the protocol functions with the level 2 at the DCE, using the HDLC protocol over the level 1 physical connection.

Establishing the link connection

An earlier specification of the X.25 protocol included a lever 2 initialisation procedure called LAP (Link Access Protocol) This procedure has been superseded by a simpler *balanced* procedure called LAPB. The LAPB method of initialisation sets up both channels simultaneously.

Data transfer

Level 2 should provide a sequenced, error-free transport of lever 3 packers from the DTE to the DCE and vice versa. As only 3 bits are allowed for the sequence number and acknowledgement number in the C field, the maximum window size is 7. In X. 25 the link level window size is fixed when the subscriber first applies to use the network. The operation of the data transfer allows the use of limited buffers at the sender (no more than 7) and no requirement for extra buffers to handle out-of-sequence frames at the receiver. The cost of the small buffer requirement is extra channel capacity taken up with retransmission.

The use of X.25 to connect hosts to networks would normally involve a fairly high-speed circuit between the DTE and DCE The limiting factor in performance is more likely to be the network and level 3, so a superefficient level 2 is not necessary; thus simpler techniques, such as Go-Back-N, can be used. The transfer of sequenced frames of information is straightforward but what makes the operation complex (and this applies to every protocol) is the handling of exceptions and errors. There are two basic errors that can occur during data transfer.

1. The frame check sequence indicates an error in the packet.
2. The packet appears to contain no transmission errors but the contents of the A and C fields are not those expected.

In case 1 above the frame is thrown away and no further action is taken by the receiver. Obviously when a frame is discarded the next frame received is not the one expected. In case 2 there are a number of inconsistencies that can be classed as errors. The most common would be a sequence error where a previous packet had been lost or discarded. To ensure that the frame sequence is maintained at the receiver, any frame that does not contain a sequence number matching that of the next expected frame variable, V(R), is an error. If the sequence number of the error frame is within the window, the receiver returns an REJ response to indicate, in the N(R) field, the frame from which the sender should retransmit.

If the frame sequence number is not within the window then the sequence numbers of the two ends have become unsynchronised. The only way to recover from a synchronisation problem is to reset the sender and receiver to a known state. The CMDR (command reject) frame initiates a reset which is completed by going through the link establishment exchange. After a reset, the two end-stations will be in a known, initial state. The reset procedure is used to recover from all errors other than the loss of an information frame. A reset may be caused by the receipt of a command or response that is not expected; for instance, a UA if the data transfer is in progress, or the setting of the P/F bit in a response when no command has been sent with that bit set. The RNR (receiver not ready) frame tells the data sender that the receiver will ignore any further information frames (flow control stop). Once the receiver has returned an RNR response to an information frame, no more information frames are accepted, but the *N(R)* field in the header of any further information frames is inspected so that information frames in the opposite direction are properly acknowledged.

The RNR response only stops information on one channel; the other channel is unaffected. When the receiver has more buffer space, an RR (receiver ready) frame is sent to inform the information sender on that channel that more information frames may be transmitted (flow control go), starting at *N(R)*. Note that both RNR and RR have acknowledgement numbers, *N(R)*. The RR frame has another use: if the receiving station does not have any information frames to be sent on the opposite channel, the acknowledgements cannot be piggybacked, and the RR frame is then used to acknowledge the information frames. A receiver, especially a DCE (node), may not have enough buffers to take a full window for every level 2 link to which it is connected. Instead a statistical allocation could be used which assumes that not all links will be fully active at the same time and that the data is forwarded within a given time.

When the network becomes busy this allocation means that a receiver may run out of buffers and need to use some technique to stop the flow of data from one or more links. Every frame, whether it is data or control, needs some buffer space for its receipt. If all the buffers are used up by one link then none of the other links will be able to continue transferring information. Also, if every buffer is allocated, there may be no more buffers to receive a control frame acknowledging a data frame and releasing buffer space! To avoid these problems, complex buffer allocation methods may be used. Normally, enough free buffers are always kept to receive at least one frame on each link so that control information can be exchanged even if data cannot. An information frame would be received, the control information used (for example *N(R)*), and then the frame discarded so that the buffer may be used again. The loss of information frames as a result of buffer starvation means that information is lost not only because of errors in transmission, but also because of the internal operation of the nodes of a network, especially when the network becomes heavily loaded.

Link disconnection

The LAPB procedure for closing a link requires an exchange of a DISC command and a UA response. The poll/final bit is used to obtain synchronisation between the DCE and DTE.

The function of level 2 is to carry a level 3 packet across a link. The function of the network level is to carry a piece of information from one host (DTE) to another via intermediate network nodes. The transfer of the level 3 information will involve a number of level 2 links.

The X. 25 specification only covers the link between the DTE and DCE, but we will assume a similar protocol is used between each node of the network as well. Each level 3 packet contains a certain amount of level 3 protocol information in a header, and possibly some user data (from the transport level).

The major differences between levels 2 and 3 are the use of addresses and logical channel numbers. Most hosts will be connected to the network by one level 2 link. This link then has to be used to enable the host to communicate with several other hosts by multiplexing logical channels on to the one physical link. Level 3 is used to achieve this multiple connection via a single link. Using level 3 a host establishes a logical channel to another host by making a connection request using the full address of the remote host. When the connection is established it becomes a logical channel with a unique number, the logical channel number.

The logical channel number is unique only for each link. Using the logical channel concept, packets for several calls may pass across the same level 2 link as they are all identified by the unique channel number. At the DCE the channel number is used to decide which route the packet will take. The logical channel is in fact a virtual circuit.

The network level has the same basic functions to perform as the link level.

1. Connection establishment.
2. Data transfer.
3. Connection disconnection.

The difference for the network level is that these functions are now carried out (apparently) between two hosts.

Packet format

The X.25 level 3 headers are used to contain a variety of information, so they are not of uniform size like the level 2 frame headers. The level 3 headers are different for every type of packet, which makes the format quite complex. The general format identifier (GFI) field indicates which format of level 3 header follows.

The logical channel group number and logical channel number provide a 12 bit channel-numbering field. Splitting the field may allow subdivisions to be used for, say, different services. Call request and incoming call packets contain the address of the remote host (DTE). The addresses may contain fields indicating a particular process on a host as well as identifying a host. The address fields are of variable length, preceded by a byte count.

Connection establishment

To begin a call, a host uses the full address of the remote host in a call request packet sent from the DTE to the DCE. The DCE will respond with either a call accepted packet if the request was successful, or a clear indication packet if the call was refused. At the remote host the DCE will send an incoming call packet to the host to indicate that a remote call has been requested. The DTE receiving an incoming call packet will inspect the header to decide if the call is to be established or not. If the call is accepted a call accept packet is sent to the DCE; if the call is rejected a clear request is sent to the DCE. The channel number chosen for a new outgoing call by the DTE is the lowest available number.

The channel number for an incoming call is chosen by the DCE as the highest available number. If the DTE and DCE agree on the channel numbers, and the DCE will accept the call, all subsequent packets on that call will only use that channel number, not the full address. A call has been established to a remote DTE when a host receives a call accepted packet having the same channel number as the call request packet. The call is established at the remote DTE when the call accepted packet is sent to the remote DCE.

Information transfer

Level 3 transfers data to the network in a sequenced stream using Go-Back-N ARQ. The techniques of sequence numbers, piggybacked acknowledgements, RNR, RR and REJ responses are the same as for level 2, but they control the data flow across the network and into the remote host for each, independent logical channel.

The use of windows and sequence numbers was for error control in level 2 as the level 1 link was prone to errors. At level 3 the level 2 link is assumed to be error free so. the emphasis is different. The windows and sequence numbers are now used primarily for end-to-end flow control.

The receipt of acknowledgements allows more information into the network, while the window limits the number of data packets in flight at any one time. Complete suspension of the data flow can be achieved by using a level 3 RNR, but the flow can be partially adjusted by the rate of acknowledgement.

Interrupt

An extra mechanism is used at level 3 to handle what is known as *out-of-band* transmission. Normal user data on an X.25 virtual call is kept in strict sequence; this is called *in band* transmission. However, a user application often requires a special signal which is not subject to the normal flow control. Such a signal is the abort character which a terminal user would type to stop a runaway program. X.25 level 3 uses an interrupt packet to carry this out-of-band signal.

The interrupt is not subject to the normal information flow control, the idea being that the interrupt could overtake information packets already in the network. The interrupt packet contains a field to indicate the cause of the interrupt; it is up to the application to decide what to do both with the interrupt and any subsequent data. When the DTE sends an interrupt packet the DCE responds with an interrupt confirmation. The interrupt sequence is shown in figure 9.10. X.25 permits only one interrupt to be outstanding on a logical call at any one time.

Resets and restarts

In level 2 the reset was introduced as a mechanism for recovering from a protocol error where the two ends in the link became unsynchronised. The same thing can happen between the DTE and DCE at level 3, except that there are two areas where problems may occur. The first problem is due to the information frames and sequence numbers becoming out of synchronisation on a single call. This may be detected by receiving a sequence number outside the window or an acknowledgement for a packet that was not sent. An error may also have been detected by a higher-level protocol, perhaps because of a network failure. In these cases only the one logical channel is affected so a *reset* is used. This sets the level 3 sequence numbers to 0 at the DTE and DCE. The reset will also be propagated to the remote DTE-DCE pair. The reset can be initiated from either the DTE or DCE and requires the usual request-confirmation exchange. A reset may cause the loss of any information packets within the network so a higher-level protocol will need to recover any lost data. More drastic action is needed if the DTE and DCE become unsynchronised over global level 3 operation. An example is the choice of a channel number for a call request. If the DCE does not agree with the DTE over the chosen channel number (it should be the lowest free number) it means one of them thinks it has more logical calls opened than the other! The freeing of logical channel numbers correctly is the reason for the clear-request and clear-confirmation pair. When the whole level 3 needs resynchronisation a restart is initiated. This affects all the logical channels on the DTE-DCE link. A reset on the level 2 link is propagated as a restart at level 3.

Call disconnection

A DTE wishing to terminate a call issues a clear request packet, to which the DCE will respond with a clear confirmation packet when the call has been cleared in the DCE. This may involve waiting for the forwarding of any information packets still held there. When the clear confirmation is received the channel number is freed for further use. At the remote end the DCE wit send a clear indication packet indicating that the remote host has closed, and no more information packets will follow. The remote DTE will respond with a clear confirmation packet when all outstanding information packets have been acknowledged.

Data flow

The level 3 transport mechanism requires the data from the higher-level protocols to be broken into packets for transfer across the DTE-DCE interface. The X.25 recommendation specifies possible data lengths of 128 256, 512 and 1024 bytes, where 128 is the preferred maximum. It is probable that the PTT networks will guarantee 128 byte data packets. This means a user message must be broken into 128 byte sequences, the last one being perhaps less than 128 bytes. To enable the receiver to reassemble a message from multiple packets, level 3 uses a *more data bit* (M) in the information packet header to indicate that the current packet is not the last one of a message.

Just as the level 2 and level 3 need to include control information in the frames and packets as well as information from the next higher level, it is likely that a higher-level protocol would like to send control and data over level 3. The higher-level protocol may decide to add the control bits to the front of messages it passes to level 3. However, level 3 provides a mechanism that allows a higher-level protocol to multiplex data and control information on to the level 3 packet stream, thus maintaining the sequence of data and control across the network. This mechanism is the Q *bit.* The Q bit is set when the packet contains control information, and is clear when the packet contains data. Thus the higher-level protocol can quickly separate control and data information when receiving level 3 packets.

X.25 implementation

An advantage claimed for X.25 is that it only describes the host-to-node (DTE-to-DCE) interface. The network itself (internode) can use any convenient protocols, even completely different protocols, and the user would be unaware of them. In fact the proposed PTT networks are all planning to use X.25, or variations, within the networks for node-to-node transfer. The problem considered here is the implications of two methods of implementing an X.25 interface in a DCE that produce quite different results for the user. The discussion will show that even standards have complex problems of *meaning* (or semantics).

The two methods of implementation involve the mechanism for generating responses to various DTE packets at level 3. From the above description it can be seen that a command response sequence is used throughout level 3. The X.25 specification indicates quite clearly what responses are required, but leaves it up to the implementer to decide when, and under what criteria, the responses are made.

Consider the implementation that produces the DCE response as soon as the DTE's packet has been processed at the (local) DCE. This means the DCE's answer is sent to the DTE at the same time as the original request is forwarded across the network and well in advance of its arrival at the remote DTE. Such an implementation would give a very quick response to the user host. For instance, as data is passed to the DCE it is acknowledged immediately, even before it has crossed the network. The DCE-DTE flow control would ensure the DCE was not flooded with data, but large amounts could be in transit within the network before the call has been established at the remote end. This implementation would give the host the appearance of high throughput, as the DCE-DTE flow control would be the only restraint. If the DTE receives a level 3 acknowledgement for a data packet, does this mean that the remote DTE has received it, or only that the local DCE has? To be consistent in this implementation it would have to be the latter, so the DCE has taken on the responsibility for delivery of that data. A higher-level protocol would be needed, with its own flow control, to handle the host-to-host transfer.

This implementation has the effect, mentioned above, of apparently providing a fast throughput. A host may be able to open a call (to the local DCE), send data, and close the call, before the remote DTE has received any data. The network, however, will contain a large amount of unacknowledged packets as the DTE-DCE flow control will accept packets as fast as the DCE can forward them into the network. This makes end-to-end flow control in the network difficult and can quickly lead to congestion.

In the second implementation we only allow the DCE to respond to the DTE when the response from the remote DTE has been received by the local DCE. Data sent from the DTE is not acknowledged until the remote DTE has accepted the packet. This gives the host an impression of a long delay. In fact the delay is the round trip to the remote host, plus processing. This end-to-end use of the level 3 protocol reduces the amount of processing required from higher-level protocols.

The sending DTE will only be able to have a window of packets outstanding which will represent the maximum number of data buffers which the whole network will need for the call. This makes the resource management within the network easier and is less likely to produce congestion. The cost is the lower performance seen by the user. Each packet takes longer to be acknowledged, thus reducing the throughput. There is also the problem of gaps which occurs when a window full of packets is sent rapidly, which is followed by a delay until the first acknowledgement comes back. This *bursty* mode of operation gives the network an uneven response and is difficult for both the host and DCE to manage.

In Internet, network management was done using the *Simple Gateway Monitoring Protocol* (SGMP). Then the *Simple Network Management Protocol* (SNMP) was defined for the management of networks and network devices. However, the syntax and semantics of SNMP are different from those of SGMP. The objects to be managed are defined in the *management information base* (MIB). These objects must follow a certain set of rules as mentioned in the *Structure of Management Information (SMI)* such that an object defined by the X group is compatible with the definition of the object by the Y group.

Objects in Internet and those in OSI are different. Internet objects are similar to attributes in OSI, and an Internet object group can best be described as analogous to an OSI managed object class. In Internet, an object is more like a variable found in programming languages; it has a syntax and semantics. Each object can have one or more object instances, each of which, in turn, has one or more values.

The network management system consists of one or more *network management stations* (NMSs) and one or more *network elements* (NEs) with network management functions, management information, and management protocols. The concepts of manager and agent are relatively new in Internet network management. An NMS is analogous to a manager in concept, and the network management functions of NEs are rolled into agents. NMSs have the following primary functions:

- Retrieve values of objects in NEs using agents. This management operation is done by a Get.
- Change or alter the values of objects in NEs using agents. This can be done by a Set.

Network management functions are responsible for monitoring and controlling the managed nodes. SNMP provides the management protocol for network management in the Internet world. The application entities, which can be manager or agent, exchange management information. These application entities are known as SNMP application entities. NMS sends requests and receives responses from the agents. They can also receive notifications known as *traps.* A trap is an unsolicited message sent from an agent. Agents reside in NEs, which are also sometimes known as *managed nodes.* These managed nodes are devices such as hosts, routers, LAN adapters, modems, multiplexers, hubs, and printers. Agents have the following important functions:

— They are instrumented to retrieve management information from the objects, which represent the resources.

— They alter the values of objects.

— They receive responses and traps and send them, in turn, to network management stations.

SNMP is used to communicate management information between a management station and the agents. The management applications are built on the top of network management stations. Some key philosophies involved in the design of SNMP are as follows:

— The management protocol should be as simple as possible and must be provided at least cost. The management protocols should have bare-minimum operations.

— Network management must be robust and able to provide the services, even when the state of the network is not quite reliable or when there are too many errors. SNMP must be able to handle the worst-case scenarios.

— The standard MIB will have core objects defined, and new objects to cover managed devices or managed nodes should be added to the MIB as needed. This extensibility should be easy.

— In the workload distribution between the NMS and the agents in the managed nodes, the major workload will be off-loaded to the NMS, such that it will be easy to add new managed nodes to the network. This will also help the easy extensibility of the managed nodes supported.

— The transport used for carrying management protocols is connectionless UDP. It is not necessary to have the facilities provided by a connection-oriented transport, because they add complexity to the transport.

— The initial objective was to have easy migration to the OSI network management. Now, due to the popularity of SNMP, this objective is in question. Some proponents of SNMP support abandoning the ultimate migration to OSI and, instead, favor the independent growth of Internet network management.

Index